高校英语选修课系列教材

新编听说进阶
——中高级英语听说教程
（第三版）

何福胜 编

清华大学出版社
北京

内 容 简 介

《新编听说进阶——中高级英语听说教程》（第三版）是在2009年出版的《新编听说进阶（修订版）》基础上，参考《大学英语教学指南》和《研究生英语教学要求》所编写的一本中、高级英语听说教材。全书包括18个主单元、2个听力测试和1套实用英语口语测试题，配有近5个小时的音频资料。教程的设计着力于提高学生的听力技能和口语表达能力。本教程的特点是选材内容新颖，题材广泛，语言规范，练习设计活泼多样，融趣味性、挑战性、思想性为一体，尤其注重与中国国情和中国学生的具体情况相结合。录音材料讲究真实性，语速自然，循序渐进，内含200多人的不同声音和口音。本书配套的所有音频资料，可登录ftp://ftp.tup.tsinghua.edu.cn（外语分社）下载，下载密码咨询电话：010-62794309。

本书适合已具有大学英语四级水平的学生使用，也可用于听说强化训练和学术交流培训。

版权所有，侵权必究。举报：010-62782989，beiqinquan@tup.tsinghua.edu.cn。

图书在版编目（CIP）数据

新编听说进阶：中高级英语听说教程 / 何福胜编. —3版. —北京：清华大学出版社，2017
（2025.1重印）
（高校英语选修课系列教材）
ISBN 978-7-302-46141-8

Ⅰ.①新… Ⅱ.①何… Ⅲ.①英语–听说教学–高等学校–教材 Ⅳ.①H319.9

中国版本图书馆CIP数据核字（2017）第007821号

责任编辑：刘细珍
封面设计：平　原
责任校对：王凤芝
责任印制：杨　艳

出版发行：清华大学出版社
网　　址：https://www.tup.com.cn，https://www.wqxuetang.com
地　　址：北京清华大学学研大厦A座　　邮　编：100084
社 总 机：010-83470000　　邮　购：010-62786544
投稿与读者服务：010-62776969，c-service@tup.tsinghua.edu.cn
质量反馈：010-62772015，zhiliang@tup.tsinghua.edu.cn

印 装 者：三河市人民印务有限公司
经　　销：全国新华书店
开　　本：185mm×260mm　　印　张：17　　字　数：375千字
版　　次：2004年8月第1版　2017年2月第3版　印　次：2025年1月第6次印刷
定　　价：69.00元

产品编号：072004-02

前　言

《新编听说进阶——中高级英语听说教程》（第三版）是在 2009 年出版的《新编听说进阶（修订版）》基础上，参考《大学英语教学指南》和《研究生英语教学要求》所编写的一本中、高级英语听说教材。本书自第一版出版至今已有十多年，被数十所院校采用，并一直是清华大学等高校研究生英语课程主干教材，很受学生欢迎。此次修订增加了一些新的素材，修订了部分内容和练习设计，使之更富有时代感，更能与中国的现实情况相结合，基本能够满足学生对英语听说交际技能和国际学术交流能力的需求。

本书在编排上将录音书面材料和听力练习答案附在书中，这样可以帮助学生自学和掌握语言点。其匹配的音频资料共有近 5 个小时*，内含 200 多人的声音和口音。全书包括 18 个主单元、2 个听力测验和 1 套实用英语口语试题。每个单元一般需要 2 个课时。教师可以根据学生的具体情况对授课内容进行适当的调整。

本书每一单元可分为 3 个阶段进行教学：引导活动—听力活动—口语活动。引导活动形式多样，有听力练习、口头练习、简单问答等，其目的是将学生引导到某一单元的主题上来。引导活动也包括处理所列出的听力材料词汇，这些词汇有可能影响学生对听力材料的理解，因而应在放录音前启发学生理解其词义。听力活动包括听录音、学生讨论答案、重复听录音、检查答案等过程。口语活动是听力活动的自然延伸和发展，要求学生积极参与，教师作必要的指导。该活动结束前可安排几名学生进行示范表演，以增加活动的趣味性。在教学过程中我们发现，课堂的教学活动与课外的英语实践活动相结合能产生非常好的效果。建议任课教师重视每单元最后的课外小组活动练习，从上课一开始就将学生分为若干学习小组，每组 8 人左右，让学生自己组织课外英语实践，完成课外交流活动，并轮流在课堂上进行小组活动汇报演讲。

本书在编写过程中曾得到过多位人士的大力支持和协助，在此一并致谢。编者在选编教程时参考并选用了部分国外教材和其他英语有声资料中的一些内容。这些材料涉及面较广，在此不一一注明，谨向所有有关人士深表谢意。

由于编者水平有限，编写时间仓促，书中定有疏忽和错误之处，敬请广大使用者批评指正。

编　者

2016 年 7 月于清华园

---

* 本书配套的所有音频资料，可登录 ftp://ftp.tup.tsinghua.edu.cn（外语分社）下载，下载密码咨询电话：010-62794309。

Instructions for Use

New Progressive Listening and Speaking (Third Edition) is a book of listening and speaking activities for intermediate and upper-intermediate students of English. There are 18 main units, 2 listening tests and 1 oral test. Each main unit is based on a different topic or theme, within which there are three or more listening comprehension tasks and some speaking activities, which are designed to stimulate students to share their ideas, opinions and experiences with each other. The topics selected are practical and realistic, and meet students' need at this stage of study and want to talk about in English. The activities and tasks designed in this book are also interesting, challenging, and more importantly, relevant to the students themselves.

English is a language that is spoken not just in Britain, but all over the world—often as a means of communication between people who have no other language in common. The activities in this book don't attempt to prepare learners for "life in Britain or America" but for using English as an international language. During the course, however, some background knowledge of these two chief English-speaking countries is also presented and practised at many points. This is intended to prepare students in some way to live or work in an English speaking situation in the future.

New Progressive Listening and Speaking (Third Edition) can also be used as a complementary part to any reading and writing course, e.g. for post-CET-4 and CET-6 English courses. And of course, it can also be used on its own as an intensive "refresher course" or optional course for graduates as well as undergraduates who need to develop their fluency in English after they have completed their English studies at the elementary level. This book is also ideal for those pre-departure students who are on an intensive English course which prepares them to study or work in an English-speaking country.

Teachers and students are expected to select the units and activities that seem most relevant and interesting to them. For instance, Unit 1 "Personal Information" is only suitable for the first class for a group of new students who do not know each other at this point. This would not be meaningful for a class in which everybody knows everybody else very well. Again, Unit 4 "Marriage" might not be suitable for a group of adult students who are already married.

Listening Exercises

Each unit in *New Progressive Listening and Speaking* (Third Edition) has three or more listening exercises. Each listening exercise trains students' listening skills. At the same time, it provides students with a topic, a range of opinions or some information based on which students can develop their language competence at a later stage. The language and the lexical items introduced in the listening material also help students to participate more effectively in the activities that follow.

There is generally a "before", "during" and "after" phase to each listening exercise. In brief, the phases are as follows:

1. Before Listening

Learners are introduced to the situation in which each conversation takes place. They find out their purpose in listening to the recording and any background information they may need. This is generally fulfilled through some of the pre-listening exercises that are specially designed for this purpose or through questions and answers that are included in the directions of the listening exercise. It is noted that the lexical items given after each listening exercise should also be introduced at this stage. This is intended to enhance students' understanding of the recording in which these lexical items might prove problematic and therefore hamper their comprehension in the first place.

2. During Listening

Usually learners need to listen to the recording twice: the first time to understand the information and useful language expressions; and the second to check and confirm their answers to the listening tasks. These tasks may involve drawing a diagram, filling in a chart or making notes, for example. Sometimes, two listening tasks are designed on the same listening text, one to check the gist and the other the detailed information. Most often, only one listening task is designed to check both the gist and detailed information. It should be noted here that all the listening tasks used are attempted to be authentic in some ways so as to specifically train students' note-taking skills. They will also need these skills for future listening examinations.

3. After Listening

Learners compare notes or answers with their partners. They help each other in their understanding of the listening task. Then, the teacher elicits the required information from the students and makes sure they have the right answers. Usually, a second listening follows here, which gives students a chance to find out where they went wrong and what they missed in the previous listening.

Speaking Activities

In the speaking activities, students work together in pairs or in groups. Sometimes they can even move around the classroom and talk to anyone they like. The aim is to encourage students to exchange ideas and opinions with each other. In each activity students are given a purpose or task, and this makes the activities much more motivating and realistic than just "answering questions". Most of the time, since students are directed to talk about themselves or things they are familiar with, the activities tend to become more meaningful. Of course, this also makes the speaking tasks easier to do so that some students can have a go at them. Besides, the useful expressions and the lexical items introduced in the listening tasks and elicited through the pre-listening activities also help students in this way. The tasks are designed on the assumption that Chinese learners of English are generally weak in this type of productive skill—speaking. Some speaking activities also incorporate some language functions such as making one's point, giving explanations, etc.

It is noted that some sort of checking or demonstration should be an indispensable phase which follows a speaking activity. For instance, when students are supposed to make choices, the teacher could later elicit each of the students' choices and make some comments if they have made mistakes.

Group Projects

It is discovered that incorporating in-class teaching with outside-class practice can produce fairly remarkable effects for students to improve their listening and speaking skills for communication. It is suggested that students should be divided into groups of 5 or 6 in the first class. They then should have regular group meetings each week, finishing the group projects as required and making group presentations about their group work in the next class. These group projects are usually quite specific, requiring students to communicate with each other in English for at least 2 hours. It is also advisable to tell students to take charge of their group work in turns and make classroom presentations in turns as well. The first 15 minutes or so of a class can always be used for students' presentations about their group work. It is necessary for the teacher to make some comments. Don't forget encouraging comments.

The Teacher's Role

Only a rough guide is provided in this introduction. Hopefully, each teacher will use this book in his or her own way, adapting the materials to the needs of each different group of learners. The book is designed to stimulate learners and teachers alike, not to control them.

The teacher has three main things to do while using the book:

1. To get things started—making sure everyone knows what he has to do and possess the necessary vocabulary to do so.

2. To monitor the group at work, and sometimes, participate in it, and decide when to stop the activity.

3. To lead a short follow-up discussion after each activity—providing further information or making comments or doing any remedial work necessary.

Contents

Unit 1	**Personal Information** 1
	Listening One: Personal information registration 1
	Listening Two: What do you say first? 3
	Group Project 6
Unit 2	**You and Me** 7
	Listening One: I hope you don't mind my asking 7
	Listening Two: Getting to know someone 10
	Group Projects 13
Unit 3	**City and Country** 14
	Listening One: There's no place like home 14
	Listening Two: It's the only way to travel 17
	Group Projects 19
Unit 4	**Marriage** 20
	Listening One: Important tips for choosing a life partner 20
	Listening Two: A successful marriage 23
	Group Projects 26
Unit 5	**Keep in Touch** 27
	Listening One: Can I take a message? 27
	Listening Two: The dictaphone 29
	Group Projects 33
Unit 6	**Habits** 34
	Listening One: Sleeping habits 34
	Listening Two: Kicking the habit 37
	Group Projects 40

| Unit 7 | Clubs/Societies | 41 |

- Listening One: Join the club ... 41
- Listening Two: College capers ... 43
- Group Projects ... 46

| Unit 8 | Past Schooling | 47 |

- Listening One: Once upon a time ... 47
- Listening Two: A good start ... 49
- Group Projects ... 52

| Unit 9 | Past and Future | 53 |

- Listening One: It's all in the past ... 53
- Listening Two: A vision of the future ... 55
- Group Projects ... 57

| Unit 10 | Commercials/Advertisements | 59 |

- Listening One: Clensip ... 59
- Listening Two: Waverley—a holiday you'll never forget ... 60
- Group Projects ... 64

| Unit 11 | Entertainment | 65 |

- Listening One: Finding out what's going on in town ... 65
- Listening Two: This is nine o'clock news ... 67
- Group Projects ... 69

| Unit 12 | Climate and Weather | 70 |

- Listening One: Watching the weather ... 70
- Listening Two: News about the weather ... 71
- Group Projects ... 73

| Unit 13 | Accommodation | 74 |

- Listening One: The inside story ... 74
- Listening Two: This window here has a lovely view ... 77
- Group Projects ... 78

| Unit 14 | Stay Well | 79 |

- Listening One: Doctor's orders ... 79

Contents

	Listening Two: A healthy life	81
	Group Projects	83

Unit 15 What's My Line? 84
    Listening One: Willing to train 84
    Listening Two: What do you do? 87
    Group Projects 91

Unit 16 Making Your Point 92
    Listening One: Right or wrong? 92
    Listening Two: There's nothing I can do! 94
    Group Projects 96

Unit 17 Sports 97
    Listening One: Which sport? 97
    Listening Two: Sport and violence 99
    Group Projects 100

Unit 18 Going on Holiday 101
    Listening One: Holidays in the United States 101
    Listening Two: Amazing journey 103
    Group Projects 106

Listening Test 1 107
    Section One 107
    Section Two 107
    Section Three 108

Listening Test 2 109
    Section One 109
    Section Two 110
    Section Three 110

Oral Test 111

Recording Script 121

Reference Key to Listening Tasks 226

Unit 1 Personal Information

Listening One: Personal information registration

Task a Pair-work: What kind of information is personal information? What are some of the useful expressions for asking about personal information? Join a partner and discuss these two questions. Fill in the chart below with your answers.

Personal Information	Expressions for Asking About Personal Information
Name Date of birth	What's your name please? May I have your address?

Task b You are going to hear an interview that takes place at an employment agency. Listen to the recording and complete the following information about the applicant.

Full name: _____
Present job: _____
Date of birth: _____
Marital status: _____
Address: _____
Telephone No.: _____

> **Lexical items:**
> receptionist   surname

Task c In the interview, the clerk asks the applicant some questions. Listen to the recording again and write down the expressions that are used to find out the applicant's

name: _____?
present job: _____?
date of birth: _____?
marital status: _____?
address: _____?

Task d You will hear a conversation between the secretary of a language school and a new student who wants to enroll. Read the registration form below. Then listen to the recording and complete the form for the student.

Registration Form

Name: _____ Age: _____
Occupation: _____ Nationality: _____
UK Address: _____
_____

Length of course: _____
Number of hours per day: _____
Course starting date: _____
Price of course plus accommodation: _____
Accommodation: Required/not required
Amount of deposit paid: _____

School facilities: _____
Teachers: _____

> **Lexical items:**
> Youth Hostel   accommodation   a packed lunch   competitive
> cookery   pottery   entrance test   assess   deposit

UNIT **1** Personal Information

Task e **Pair-work:** Is there anyone you don't know sitting around you? Get to know him or her by exchanging your personal information. Complete the following information chart for your partner.

Personal Information Chart	
Your partner's name: _____	
Date of birth	
Address	
Hometown	
Department	
Major address	
E-mail	
Telephone number	
Marital status	

Listening Two: What do you say first?

Task a **Pair-work:** What do you say when you meet someone for the first time? What do you think people might talk to each other? Join a partner and discuss the possible topics. Make a list of these topics in the spaces provided below.

_____
_____
_____
_____

Task b When English-speaking people meet each other for the first time, they often follow a pattern. You will hear a short conversation and a short commentary on the conversation. What do the people talk about? Listen to the recording and write down the steps.

When people meet, they usually

1. _____
2. _____
3. _____

 "First impressions" are what you think when you meet someone for the first time. Your opinion is based on what the person says or does. You will hear four short conversations. What do people do to make a good first impression? Write down their strategies.

Strategies to Make a Good First Impression	
1.	
2.	
3.	
4.	

Task d Speaking: How do you get to know each other in a class or at a party? First refer to the sample answers below.

In class
This class is great.
By the way, I'm _____.
Which department are you from?
At a party
Nice party.
I'm _____. Don and I are classmates.
How do you know Don?

Now you're going to have your own conversations. Stand up. Go up to a classmate you don't know. Start a conversation using the same steps:

—Talk about something you both have in common.

—Say your name and find out your partner's name.

—Ask further questions.

Keep the conversation going for as long as possible. Exchange your

UNIT 1 Personal Information

personal information such as name, age, date of birth, hometown, address, telephone number, department, major, email address and QQ number. Then end your conversation, (for example, you may use "Excuse me, I need to talk to someone over there. It was nice meeting you.") and find a new partner and start a new conversation. Meet as many classmates as possible.

Task e Pair-work: Work in pairs and discuss the following questionnaire. Record each of your answers in the spaces provided.

A Short Questionnaire to Discover Your Own Values

As an individual you have your own values. These values generally determine what is important to you and what is not. Discuss the following list of 18 values one by one and decide on their relative importance by giving certain points under the 100 points scale (0–100).

1. Ambitious (hard-working, aspiring) _____
2. Broad-minded (open-minded) _____
3. Capable (competent, effective) _____
4. Clean (neat, tidy) _____
5. Courageous (standing for your beliefs) _____
6. Forgiving (willing to pardon others) _____
7. Helpful (working for the welfare of others) _____
8. Honest (sincere, truthful) _____
9. Imaginative (daring, creative) _____
10. Independent (self-reliant/sufficient) _____
11. Intellectual (intelligent, reflective) _____
12. Logical (consistent, rational) _____
13. Loving (affectionate, tender) _____
14. Obedient (dutiful, respectful) _____
15. Self-controlled (restrained, self-disciplined) _____
16. Polite (courteous, well-mannered) _____
17. Responsible (dependable, reliable) _____
18. Cheerful (light-hearted, joyful) _____

5

Group Project

Form groups of five or six and make appointment to have a group meeting. Each of you should make a brief introduction (of five or six minutes) about yourself at the meeting. Your introduction can cover the following personal information: name, date of birth, place of birth, address, major, family, hometown, hopes and expectations in taking this course, etc. Choose one of you as the representative of your group. This representative will have about five minutes to report to the whole class about your group project in the next class.

Unit 2 You and Me

Listening One: I hope you don't mind my asking

Task a You're going to hear part of a market survey in which different people are asked some personal questions. Before you listen to the recording, work in pairs and discuss what kind of answers each of you would give to the six questions below. Record your partner's answers.

A Questionnaire to Discover Your Personal Information

Name: _____

1. What do you enjoy most in life?
   _____

2. What is your greatest ambition?
   _____

3. What has been your greatest achievement?
   _____

4. Which person do you admire most?
   _____

5. Who do you get on with best of all?
   _____

6. What was the nicest thing that happened to you yesterday?
   _____

Task b Listen to the recording and write down the answers each of the three speakers gives to the six questions above. Try to make your notes as brief as possible.

Questions	1st Speaker	2nd Speaker	3rd Speaker
1.			
2.			
3.			
4.			
5.			
6.			

> **Lexical items:**
> hallowed   castle   awful
> super   frivolous   safari
> Far be it from me to say.

Task C You are going to hear four people answer questions for a market survey. As you listen to the recording, complete the following chart with the answers the speakers give to the questions below.

1. What do you do for a living?

2. What do you do for fun (like to do in your spare time)?

3. What is the most exciting thing that has happened to you recently?

4. Who do you admire most in this world?

5. What do you want to be doing in five years (five years from now)?

Questions	David	Suzanne	Adolfo	Linda
1.				
2.				
3.				
4.				
5.				

UNIT 2 You and Me

Lexical items:		
survey	terrific	classics
fabulous	jog	Boston Marathon
musical	Martin Luther King, Jr.	
Sophia Loren	beauty school	hang out with
pizza	stuff	beauty salon

Task d **Pair-work:** Look at the questionnaire below. First, one of you asks all the questions and the other answers them. When this has been done, change roles. In the end, decide whose answer to each question is more interesting. Refer to the useful expressions below the questionaire.

A Questionnaire to Discover Your Personal Information

Name: _____

1. What things do you dislike most in life?
   _____

2. What is the most exciting thing that's ever happened to you till now?
   _____

3. What are your top five ambitions in life?
   _____

4. What are you looking forward to most of all this year?
   _____

5. What things in life make you happy?
   _____

6. What things make you sad or angry?
   _____

7. If you could have one wish come true, what would it be?
   _____

Useful Expressions		
Getting someone's attention	Responding to the question	Responding to an answer
1. Excuse me ... Could I ask you a few questions? 2. Excuse me ... Can I interrupt you for a moment? 3. Would you mind answering a few questions? 4. I wonder if you'd mind answering a few questions for our survey?	1. Certainly. 2. Oh ... yes, all right. 3. Why not? 4. Not at all. 5. Sure. 6. No problem.	1. Oh, yes, fascinating. 2. Thank you (very much). 3. That's lovely, isn't it? 4. Really? 5. That's terrific! 6. (That's) Fabulous! 7. That's wonderful! 8. That's very exciting!

Task e **Pair-work:** What answers will you give to these five questions? Now work in pairs and ask/answer these questions. Fill in the questionnaire with your partner's answers.

A Questionnaire to Discover Your Personal Information

Name: _____

1. What do you do for a living?
   _____

2. What do you do for fun (like to do in your spare time)?
   _____

3. What is the most exciting thing that has happened to you recently?
   _____

4. Who do you admire most in this world?
   _____

5. What do you want to be doing in five years (five years from now)?
   _____

Listening Two: Getting to know someone

Task a **Pair-work:** Everybody has some good friends or relations. Work with a partner and discuss the three questions concerning friends. First one of you asks the questions and the other answers them. Change roles when this has been done.

UNIT 2 You and Me

Questions	Answers
1. How important are friends to you?	
2. What exactly do you mean by a friend?	
3. Are you very good at keeping in touch with friends if you don't see them regularly?	

Task b Martin, Robert and Jean are being interviewed on the subject of friendship. Listen to the recording and note down each of their answers to the three questions in the previous task. Make your notes as brief as possible. You only need to write down the most important information.

Questions	Martin	Robert	Jean
1.			
2.			
3.			

> **Lexical items:**
> cousin   count on   bitterness
> lose one's temper   emigrate

Task c A young man and a girl have met each other for the first time on a beach while they were on holiday in Portugal. They have talked about five topics. Listen to the recording and write down the topics.

	Topics
1.	
2.	
3.	
4.	
5.	

> **Lexical items:**
> Portugal   Sydney   marvellous
> Lisbon   freewheeling   windsurf
> coincidence

Task d Pair-work: Discuss with a partner what your relationship with your classmates was like at school and what your present relationship with your university classmates is like. Also talk about how your own relationships have changed or developed over the past years.

Task e Pair-work: Work in pairs and discuss the following questionnaire. Record your answers to the questions by ticking the boxes which correspond to your choices.

A Short Questionnaire to Discover How You Feel About Yourself

	Yes	A bit	No
1. I am quite confident when learning a new game or sport.	☐	☐	☐
2. I make a better follower than leader.	☐	☐	☐
3. I have never been a very popular person.	☐	☐	☐
4. I rarely feel self-conscious in a strange group.	☐	☐	☐
5. It is easy for me to strike up a conversation with someone.	☐	☐	☐
6. I am not the type of person one remembers after meeting for the first time.	☐	☐	☐
7. I am seldom at a loss for words.	☐	☐	☐
8. I am considered a leader in my social circle.	☐	☐	☐
9. I usually get my way in arguments.	☐	☐	☐
10. I am ill at ease when I am meeting new people.	☐	☐	☐
11. I enjoy stating my opinions in front of a group.	☐	☐	☐
12. I often wish that I were more outgoing.	☐	☐	☐
13. It's hard for me to change other people's minds.	☐	☐	☐
14. People seem to be interested in getting to know me better.	☐	☐	☐
15. I seem to do more listening than talking in conversations with others.	☐	☐	☐
16. I like to remain unnoticed when others are around.	☐	☐	☐
17. I usually try to add a little excitement to a party.	☐	☐	☐

UNIT 2 You and Me

(Continued)

	Yes	A bit	No
18. I have trouble expressing my opinion.	☐	☐	☐
19. I find it easy to introduce people.	☐	☐	☐
20. I prefer to go to social functions with a group of people so as not to stand out.	☐	☐	☐

Group Projects

1. Make an appointment for a group meeting. Each of you should make a brief introduction (of five or six minutes) about yourself at the meeting. Your introduction can cover the following personal information: interests, personalities, hopes and expectations about your future, etc. Choose one of you as the representative of your group. This representative will have about five minutes to report to the whole class about your group project in the next class.

2. Design a questionnaire for a market survey about personal information. Role play the market survey among your group members. Choose one pair from your group to role play your market survey before the whole class next time.

Unit 3 City and Country

Listening One: There's no place like home

Task a Pair-work: Everyone has some experience living in the countryside or in a city. What do you think the top five advantages are of life in a village as well as in a large city? Discuss with a partner what points you would make. Note them down in the chart below.

Advantages of Living in a Village	Advantages of Living in a Large City
1.	1.
2.	2.
3.	3.
4.	4.
5.	5.

Task b You're going to hear part of a radio discussion about village life and city life. Three people will give their opinions about the advantages of village life and city life. Listen to the recording and write down their main points.

Lexical items:
broadcaster   actress   jolly good

UNIT 3 City and Country

Advantages of Living in a Village	Advantages of Living in a Large City

Task c Pair-work: Discuss with a partner what points you would make about the disadvantages of living in a village and in a large city. Note them down in the chart below.

Disadvantages of Living in a Village	Disadvantages of Living in a Large City

Task d Jean, an American, works as a researcher for the United States Tourist Bureau. She is asking two British tourists about their opinions on New York City. Listen to the conversation and complete the questionnaire with the speakers' answers.

Lexical items:
tourist bureau   amazing   skyscraper
subway   metropolitan

United States Tourist Bureau Tourist Questionnaire		
Names	Ben	Janice
Nationality	British	British
Opinion of city		

(Continued)

United States Tourist Bureau Tourist Questionnaire		
Opinion of tourist sites		
Opinion of taxis		
Opinion of subways		
Opinion of hotels		
Name and address of hotel		

Task e **Pair-work:** Below is a questionnaire about your opinions of your local city. Join a partner and interview each other with this questionnaire. Write down your partner's answers in the spaces provided. Refer to the useful expressions below the questionnaire.

Local City Tourist Bureau Tourist Questionnaire	
Opinion of the city	
Opinion of tourist sites	
Opinion of traffic	
Opinion of hotels	
Opinion of restaurants	
Opinion of shops and stores	
Opinion of environment	
Opinion of climate	
Opinion of the people	
Opinion of education	
Opinion of crime and safety	
Opinion of entertainment	
Opinion of living standard	

UNIT 3 City and Country

Useful Expressions: Asking for Opinion	Useful Expressions: Giving Opinion
How do you like our city? What do you think of the tourist sites? What's your opinion of the traffic in the city? What about the climate? How about the shops and stores? …	It's really exciting. Not too bad. They're amazing. I love it/them. I hate it/them. They're fabulous/terrific! …

Task F Pair-work: Discuss with a partner where you (would) prefer to live: in a village or a large city? What are the reasons for your preference? Also tell each other how you plan to spend your time there.

Listening Two: It's the only way to travel

Task a Pair-work: When people travel between cities, they usually take a form of public transport, e.g. plane, train, coach, or ship. Discuss with a partner what the advantages and disadvantages are of each of these forms of transport. Record your answers in the chart below.

Forms of Transport	Advantages	Disadvantages
By plane		
By train		
By coach		
By ship		

Task b You will hear a young man from America talking with a French travel agent about the best way to travel from Paris to Frankfurt. Listen to the recording and make notes in the chart below. The French travel agent speaks English with a French accent.

	Cost	Advantages	Disadvantages
Plane			
Train			
Bus			
Car			

> **Lexical items:**
> flight   francs   good deal
> unlimited mileage   route   scenic

Task c Pair-work: Work in pairs and discuss the following questionnaire. Record each of your answers in the spaces provided.

A Short Questionnaire to Discover Your Own Values

As an individual you have your own values. These values generally determine what is important to you and what is not. Discuss the following list of 18 values one by one and decide on their relative importance by giving certain points under the 100 points scale (0–100).

1. A comfortable life (a prosperous life) _____
2. An exciting life (a stimulating, active life) _____
3. A sense of accomplishment (lasting contribution) _____
4. A world at peace (free of war and conflict) _____
5. A world of beauty (beauty of nature and the arts) _____
6. Equality (brotherhood, equal opportunity) _____
7. Family security (taking care of loved ones) _____
8. Freedom (independence, free choice) _____
9. Happiness (contentedness) _____
10. Inner harmony (freedom from inner conflict) _____
11. Mature love (spiritual intimacy) _____
12. National security (protection from attack) _____
13. Pleasure (an enjoyable, leisurely life) _____

(Continued)

14. Salvation (saved eternal life) _____
15. Self-respect (self-esteem) _____
16. Social recognition (respect, admiration) _____
17. True friendship (close companionship) _____
18. Wisdom (a mature understanding of life) _____

Group Projects

1. Suppose you have got some spare cash (RMB 20,000) and two weeks off. You wish to take a holiday in one or two places in China which interest you. Discuss which place(s) you would most like to visit, how you'd travel there and what you'd do and see there.

2. At the group meeting interview one another to find out the information needed in the following chart. Choose one as the representative of your group. This representative will have about five minutes to report to the whole class about your group projects in the next class.

Information About My Hometown	
Top Five Advantages	Top Five Disadvantages

Information About Our University	
Top Five Advantages	Top Five Disadvantages

Unit 4 Marriage

Listening One: Important tips for choosing a life partner

Task a Pair-work: Different people may think differently in terms of choosing a partner. What do you think are most important when you are looking for life partner? Join a partner and discuss the top ten factors that most people consider important. Make a list of these factors in the spaces provided below.

Top Ten Most Important Factors for Choosing a Life Partner	
1.	
2.	
3.	
4.	
5.	
6.	
7.	
8.	
9.	
10.	

Task b You are going to hear a conversation that takes place in a "Find Your Partner Agency". Four people will talk about their ideal husbands or

UNIT 4 Marriage

wives. Listen to the recording and note down what each of them says about his or her ideal spouse.

1. George Hayes
   His ideal wife: a) _____
                        b) _____
                        c) _____

2. Fenella Orchard
   Her ideal husband: a) _____
                        b) _____
                        c) _____
                        d) _____

3. Stella Richards
   Her ideal husband: a) _____
                        b) _____
                        c) _____

4. Albert Winterton
   His ideal wife: a) _____
                        b) _____
                        c) _____
                        d) _____

 Task c *Blind Date* is a popular TV program in some Western countries. Strange men and women are introduced to each other for the first time. Usually a man or a woman is supposed to choose among three women or men. He or she can make his or her choice by judging their answers to the questions he or she asks them. You will hear such a program in which a young woman asks three men some questions. In the end, the young woman will choose one of the men as her partner. Listen to the recording and note down the answers each of the men gives to the questions. Have a pair-work discussion: if you were the girl, which bachelor would you choose as your partner? Why or why not?

The questions asked:

1. What do you do for a living?
2. What do you like to do in your spare time?
3. What do you think is your best quality?
4. What is your least attractive characteristic?

Questions	Bachelor 1	Bachelor 2	Bachelor 3
1.			
2.			
3.			
4.			

Lexical items:

bachelor	Ace Construction Company
composer	commercial
airline pilot	gamble
Ferrari (car brand)	date
ski	hike
witty	schedule

Task d Pair-work: Suppose you are taking part in a Blind Date program and you have to ask each other some questions to help you make your choice for a partner. Ask each other the questions below and record your partner's answers in the spaces provided. Are you satisfied with each other as partners?

Questions to Be Asked for a Blind Date Program	
Questions	Partner's Answers
1. What do you wish to do for a living?	
2. What do you like to do in your spare time?	
3. What do you think is your best quality?	
4. What is your least attractive characteristic?	

Task e Pair-work: Which of the following factors do you think are the most important when choosing a partner or spouse? Discuss each of the factors in the following and put them in the order of importance.

money	success	appearance
being interesting	athletic ability	popularity
social status	intelligence	friendliness
warmth	own accommodation	
family background	filial piety	

Listening Two: A successful marriage

 Task a Most people are usually idealistic when they make expectations about their marriages. Some people may have some experiences from which everyone can learn something. You will hear an interview with Mrs. Gold who has been married three times. Complete the chart below with what you hear.

	Information
Her first husband	
Her first marriage	
Her second husband	
Her second marriage	
Her third husband	
Her third marriage	

> **Lexical items:**
> considerate   Doncaster train crash
> regain consciousness   lipstick

Task b **Pair-work:** What do you think makes a successful marriage? What are the most important things a married couple should share? Look at the following items and put them in the order of importance.

same nationality	same religion
same class/family background	same interests
same educational background	same age range

Now look at the next list and decide which qualities you think the ideal husband/wife should have. Number the qualities from 1–10. Discuss your order in pairs and say why you think some qualities are more important than others.

good with children	attractive to the opposite sex
handy about the house	a good sense of humor
intelligent and well-educated	sociable
tidy	quite well off
faithful	hard-working
considerate	easy-going

Task c Dennis is 35 and he is a successful lawyer. He says he would like to get married. Why hasn't he done so yet? Now listen to an interview with Dennis and find out the answers to the following questions:

1. Has Dennis ever met the right woman?

   _____

2. What happened with Cynthia?

   _____

3. What happened with Sarah?

   _____

4. What does Dennis look for in a wife?

   _____

> **Lexical items:**
> work out   break off the relationship
> obviously   old-fashioned
> drift into a relationship

Task d What do you know about the marriage customs in China and other countries? You will hear a professor giving a lecture about marriage. Listen to the recording and complete the chart below.

UNIT 4 Marriage

Marriage Customs	
Chinese Customs over the Years	**Traditional Hopi Culture**

Task e Pair-work: Ask your partner the following questions and record his or her answers.

Questionnaire
Chinese Romance

1. Pretend you have just introduced two good friends, male and female. How can you tell if they are interested in each other?
2. Afterward, you talk to each friend alone and find out that each found the other very attractive. What are some of the words that your male friend might use to describe your female friend? What are some words that your female friend might use to describe him?
3. What would probably happen next, if they did like each other?
4. If they began dating, describe a typical date they might go on.
5. If they went out together every weekend for a month, would you expect them to continue to date other people at the same time?
6. How could you tell that your friends were getting serious? List some of the signs.
7. How would it affect things if your friends' parents were not happy about their relationship?
8. How would your friends' relationship be affected if they were from different religions? What about if they were from different family backgrounds or different races?
9. What would your reaction be if your friend told you that they were going to live together? What would their parents' reactions be?
10. Your friends seem to really love each other. How old do you think they should be to get married? Explain your reasons.

(Continued)

11. Some of the marriages last lifelong. What do you think are the most important reasons?
12. Nowadays a large percentage of marriages end in divorce. Could you talk about some of the reasons?

Group Projects

1. At the group meeting, discuss the factors that you think are most important in choosing a partner or spouse and describe your marriage expectations with each other. Choose one of you as the representative of your group. This representative will have about five minutes to report to the whole class about the points you have made at the group meeting in the next class.

2. Organize a Blind Date program. Each of you plays one of the different roles as the girls, the bachelors, the presenter of the program. Role play the Blind Date program among your group members. Get ready to role play your program before the whole class next time.

Unit 5 Keep in Touch

Listening One: Can I take a message?

Task a **Pair-work:** Do you know how to make telephone calls in English? Who usually speaks first, the caller or the person who answers the call? What does he or she usually say? What can the caller do if the person he or she wants to speak to is not available? What should you say if you find the right person to speak to? What should you say if you hear a recorded message? Join a partner and role play the following situations. Refer to the useful expressions provided below.

Situation One: One of you is the caller and the other is the person the caller wishes to speak to.

Situation Two: One of you is the caller and the other is not the person the caller wishes to speak to.

Situation Three: You hear a recorded message which says the host is not available at the moment and would like you to leave a message.

May I speak to Mr. Brown?	Hang on./Hold on.
Is Mr. Smith there, please?	I'll put you through.
Speaking.	Extension 2345, please.
Is that John?	Good morning, Gold Star Hotel.
It's Robert.	Could I leave a message?
Who's calling, please?	Could you give him a message?
Is that you, Jo?	Who shall I say is calling?
Hold the line, please.	Thanks for ringing (calling).
May I take a message?	Could I speak to Mr. Car, please?
Just a minute.	Let me get a pen. All right, go ahead.
I'm sorry, but he's not available.	Sure. I'll give him the message.
Is Mr. Smith in, please?	OK, this is Danny Silver and my number is 364-0107.
Shall I get him to ring (call) you?	Could you ask him to call me back?

🎧 **Task b**   You are going to hear several telephone calls. A secretary is taking phone messages for her boss who is at a meeting right now. Listen to the calls and briefly note down the messages in the spaces below.

Message 1

_____

Message 2

_____

Message 3

_____

Message 4

_____

Message 5

_____

Lexical items:		
reschedule	hold on	Puerto Rico
Pan Am (airliner)	in regard to	

🎧 **Task c**   You are going to hear one side of four telephone conversations. Listen to the recording and decide who each speaker is talking to and what he or she is talking about.

Who Is the Speaker Talking to?	What Are They Talking About?
1.	
2.	
3.	
4.	

Lexical items:		
Horizon(car brand)	Go ahead!	scene
get stuck	Watch it! (Be careful!)	drive me crazy
authority	She's stuck up.	

UNIT 5 Keep in Touch

Task d Pair-work:

Student A: You saw the poster below on the campus. You need a bike, but you can afford to pay only 80 yuan. Telephone the number given in the poster and find out more about the bike:
— How old is the bike?
— What size is it?
— What color is it?
— Has it had major repairs? etc.

You can also discuss the price. Make an appointment to see and try the bike.

> **For Sale**
> used bike—good condition
> 100 yuan or near
> Call at 4329

Student B: You have put out a poster to sell your bike. It is three years old and has been quite reliable. You have changed new tyres for the bike just recently. You are selling it because you have graduated and are leaving for another city in a couple of days. No one has called yet. Tell the first caller that you are willing to discuss the price and persuade him or her to come over to look at the bike.

Listening Two: The dictaphone

Task a A dictaphone is a recording machine used by people who wish to dictate work to be typed by their secretary. Molley Keaveny runs a small nursing agency in Dublin. The agency recruits staff for hospitals overseas, particularly the Middle East. When Molley cannot be in the office, she leaves messages and instructions on a dictaphone for her secretary. Listen to the recording and make notes of what Molley's secretary has to do today.

	What to Do
1.	
2.	
3.	
4.	
5.	
6.	

> Lexical items:
> MEDCO Clinic, Jeddah   original
> passport-sized photograph   twit
> *Nursing Weekly*   Kuwait
> *Dental Nurse*   Saudi Riyal
> Riyadh, Saudi Arabia

🎧 **Task b**   You will hear four dialogues on the telephone between a secretary and a person who is making an appointment to see someone. Listen to the recording and complete the notes below for the secretary, to include the name, the day and the time. The four callers are: James Smith, Anne Brown, Richard Jones, and David Sim.

1.	Note for Mr. Donaldson: _____ is coming to see you on _____ at _____ .
2.	Note for Professor Freeman: _____ is coming to see you on _____ at _____ .
3.	Note for Dr. Nelson: _____ is coming to see you on _____ at _____ .
4.	Note for Mrs. Harper: _____ is coming to see you on _____ at _____ .

🎧 **Task c**   You are going to hear six short conversations. From the way the people speak, can you work out what they are talking about and what the relationships are between them? Fill in the chart below with your answers (or guesses).

UNIT 5 Keep in Touch

	Speaker A	Speaker B	Topic or Purpose of Conversation
1.			
2.			
3.			
4.			
5.			
6.			

Lexical items:
authorize   credit note   expel   form
delicious   dead easy   charge

Task d Pair-work: Suppose you are in the following situations. Make telephone calls between the two of you and exchange the information needed.
1. One of you wants to find out the opening hours of the school library. The other works in the library.
2. One of you wants to find out the train schedule for another city. The other knows the information.
3. One of you wants to know the arrangement (time, duration, cost, etc.) for an English course. The other works in the language school.
4. One of you wants to book two tickets for a flight to another city. The other works in the ticket office.

Task e Pair-work: Discuss the following questions and answers in pairs and decide on your choices.

Questionnaire
Are You a Good Guest?

Tick the choices A, B or C in answer to these questions. And then CHECK YOUR SCORE.

(Continued)

1. You are invited out to dinner and are offered something to which you are allergic. Do you ...
   A   refuse politely and explain briefly?
   B   eat it, being prepared to suffer later?
   C   refuse and explain in detail?

2. You are at a party. Your host says, "I want you to meet Brian. You've both got such a lot in common." Do you ...
   A   take an instant dislike to Brian?
   B   try to find out what it is you've got in common?
   C   wait for Brian to start the conversation?

3. You are at an extremely boring party. Do you ...
   A   disappear while your host /hostess is talking to someone else?
   B   say "Thanks for a lovely evening but I have to get an early night"?
   C   ask someone else to make your excuses and go?

4. Your boyfriend/girlfriend takes you to supper with some people you haven't met before. They are all non-smokers. Do you ...
   A   light a cigarette without saying anything?
   B   ask if anyone minds if you smoke?
   C   wait till you get home before you have a cigarette?

5. You are on your way to dinner with friends of your parents when your bike breaks down. Do you ...
   A   telephone and explain why you'll be late?
   B   arrive late full of apologies?
   C   go home and phone the next day?

6. You find yourself at a small intimate party with someone with whom you have recently had a violent row (quarrel). Do you ...
   A   make an excuse and go home?
   B   ignore the person completely?
   C   join in the conversation as naturally as possible?

7. You're having tea with some older friends. They proudly hand you about sixty rather dull pictures they took on holiday. Do you ...
   A   shuffle through them as quickly as possible?
   B   show interest and ask questions about them?
   C   say that you've left your glasses at home?

UNIT 5 Keep in Touch

(Continued)

8. You break a valuable vase at a friend's house. Do you ...
   A offer to replace it and leave as soon as possible?
   B offer to replace it and help clean the mess?
   C pretend it wasn't your fault?

CHECK YOUR SCORE

1. A 10 B 5   C 0   2. A 0   B 10 C 5
3. A 0   B 10 C 5   4. A 0   B 5   C 10
5. A 10 B 5   C 0   6. A 5   B 0   C 10
7. A 0   B 10 C 5   8. A 5   B 10 C 0

If you scored a total of:
0–30   You're a terrible guest! You'll find you are not invited back.
30–50   You're a pleasant guest but you don't make a lot of effort to be friendly.
50–80   You're an excellent guest! You'll find yourself in great demand.

Group Projects

1. At the group meeting, complete the four telephone conversations (work out the other person's response in each telephone conversation) in Task c, Listening One. Role play the four conversations among your group members. Choose one pair from your group to role play a typical telephone conversation before the whole class next time.

2. In Task a, Listening Two, the boss firstly dictated a letter for the secretary to type. This is a typical business letter, informing someone of a good piece of news. First dictate the letter by listening to the recording. Then type the letter in the right business letter format. You are required to submit the letter in the next class.

Unit 6 Habits

Listening One: Sleeping habits

Task a Look carefully at this questionnaire. Tick or write down your answers.

What Are Your Sleeping Habits?
A Short Questionnaire to Discover Your Sleeping Habits

1. How much time do you spend on bed-making?
   a. 5 minutes a day
   b. 5 minutes every other day
   c. 5 minutes a week
2. Before you go to bed, do you ...?
   a. close the curtains   b. read   c. eat
3. After a night's sleep, do you find that the covers ...?
   a. are as tidy as when you went to bed
   b. are all over the floor
   c. are in a heap in the middle of the bed
4. If you have trouble getting to sleep, do you ...?
   a. count sheep
   b. toss and turn
   c. lie still and concentrate
5. If you wake up in the middle of the night, is it because ...?
   a. you remember something you ought to have done
   b. you're cold
   c. you're hungry

UNIT 6 Habits

(Continued)

6. If you hear a bump in the night, do you ...?
    a. get up cautiously and investigate quietly
    b. charge around the house with a gun
    c. turn over and go back to sleep
7. Do other people complain about your sleeping habits?
    a. never
    b. frequently
    c. sometimes
8. When you have dreams, are they mostly ...?
    a. dreams about work
    b. nightmares
    c. sweet dreams

Task b You will now hear a recorded interview with this questionnaire. Note down the answers which are given to the eight questions. If an answer happens to be one of the three choices provided in the questionnaire, simply note down a, b, or c.

Questions	Answers
1.	
2.	
3.	
4.	
5.	
6.	
7.	
8.	

Lexical items:
grateful   personal   decent   duvet
flake out   mess around   wrinkle

Task c   You will now hear a second version of the interview. This time the interviewer does not ask all the questions and they are not in the same order as in the printed questionnaire. Note down the answers given.

Questions	Answers
6.	
4.	
2.	
8.	
1.	
7.	

Lexical items:
tropical   flock   extraordinary
snore   co-operative

Task d   You will hear an interview between a doctor and a woman who has sleeping problems. Listen to the recording and take notes using the outline below.

What is the woman's personal experience with sleep?
_____

How serious a problem is sleep deprivation?
_____

Example 1: _____
Example 2: _____

How does the woman feel without sleep?
_____

What happens by Friday?
_____
_____

UNIT 6 Habits

> **Lexical items:**
> priority   accumulate   cranky
> The Exxon Valdez (a ship)

Task e   **Pair-work:** Now one of you should interview the other by using the questionnaire in Task a. Change roles when this has been done. Each of you should also note down the answers the other gives.

Listening Two: Kicking the habit

Task a   This part is about cigarette smoking: why people start and how difficult it is to give it up. You are going to hear some people talking about when and why they started smoking. Note down their answers as you listen to the recording.

	When	Why
Steve		
Miriam		
Anne		
John		

> **Lexical items:**
> draw   hooked   socially
> embarrassing   dead give-away   cancer
> foolishly   equivalent   drug
> sophisticated

Task b   You will hear different people giving reasons for or ways of giving up smoking. Note down each of their points as you listen to the recording.

Names	Reasons for or Ways of Giving up Smoking
1. Liz	
2. Miriam	
3. Alison	
4. Anne	
5. Muriel	
6. Cecil	
7. Miriam	

Lexical items:

pregnant	shilling	bloody
"Blow that!"	festivity	laryngitis
props	nasty	incentive

Task c Pair-work: All of the people you listened to have given up or tried to give up smoking. Discuss with a partner and work out some other possible ways of encouraging people to give it up. What do you think of each of them? Which are the most effective?

Task d Pair-work: Interview each other with the following questionnaire and record your partner's answers by taking notes.

Questionnaire
Good Manners in China

Your partner's name: _____

1. Imagine that you are invited to a small dinner to celebrate the graduation of a good friend. Do you bring along something to eat or drink? Explain.

2. You bring your friend a gift for his graduation. Will he open it during the party? Explain.

UNIT 6 Habits

(Continued)

3. At the party, your friend introduces you to his cousin, a woman doctor who is about 23 years old. Do you call her by her first name? Explain.

4. Your friend's cousin invites you to a party at her house next week, but you know that you will be busy then. Do you tell her that you will come anyway, just to be polite? Explain.

5. Do you ask your host for a drink if you are thirsty? Explain.

6. Do you light up a cigarette if you feel like smoking? Explain.

7. Your friend has a very nice house. Do you ask him how much it cost? Explain.

8. Dinner is served and everyone sits down. Do you begin to eat? Explain.

9. The food is delicious, but you are not really hungry. Do you eat anyway, to be polite?

10. One of the dishes is wonderful, and you would like to try a little more. Do you ask for it?

11. If your host asks you if you want more to eat, do you first say no, to be polite? Explain.

(Continued)

12. After dinner, do you help your host take the dishes out to the kitchen, to be polite? Explain.

13. After eating, everyone leaves the table to relax. Are you shocked when your host sits down and puts his feet up on a nearby chair? Explain.

14. Several days after the party, you want to tell your friend what a good time you had. Would you stop by his house without calling first? Explain.

Group Projects

1. Do you have any bad habits? How can you kick those habits? At the group meeting, discuss these questions with your group members and give some suggestions to each other to kick off these habits. Choose one of you as the representative of your group. This representative will have about five minutes to report to the whole class about the points you have made at the group meeting in the next class.

2. Design a questionnaire for a market survey about your daily habits. Role play the market survey among your group members. Choose one pair from your group to role play your market survey before the whole class next time.

Unit 7 Clubs/Societies

Listening One: Join the club

Task a Pair-work: Clubs and societies here refer to students' social groups in a college or university. Clubs and societies are one of the most important parts of the students' lives in the West countries. Below is a short questionnaire about clubs and societies concerning your undergraduate experiences. Join a partner and interview each other with this questionnaire. Record your partner's answers in the spaces provided.

A Short Questionnaire About Clubs and Societies
Undergraduate Experiences

Your partner's name: _____

1. Which university did you study in as an undergraduate?
   _____

2. Were you active in students' society activities?
   _____

3. Which societies were you a member of?
   _____

4. What did you do as a member of these societies?
   _____

5. What problems did you come across in your society activities?
   _____

6. What did you benefit from these society activities?
   _____

7. What comment can you make on the clubs and societies in your university?
   _____

🎧 **Task b** You are going to hear the President of a student society introducing her club to new students. Listen to the recording and write down the following information about the club.

Notes about the club:

Name: _____
Number of present members: _____
Began in (year): _____
Objectives: 1) _____
_____

2) _____
_____

3) _____
_____

Membership fee: _____
Rights of members: _____

Lexical items:
portable camera   studio camera
editing suite   magazine type program

 Task c You are going to hear three heads of college societies introducing their clubs to a group of new students. Complete the chart below as you listen to the recording.

	Society 1	Society 2	Society 3
Name			
Objectives			
Locations/ Times of meetings			
Past record			
Plans			

UNIT 7 Clubs/Societies

Lexical items:			
location	perspective	awareness	stereo room
disc	current trend	band	venue
drama	rehearse	assembly room	up to date

Task d Pair-work: You now have some information about four different clubs or societies: The Video Club, The Historical Society, The Pop Music Society, and The Drama Society. Discuss the questions below with a partner and exchange your ideas.
1. Which of these societies would you like to join?
2. Why do you make such a choice?
3. What do you expect to do as a member of the society?

Listening Two: College capers

Task a Pair-work: Below is a questionnaire about clubs and societies in your present university. Join a partner and interview each other with this questionnaire. Record your partner's answers in the spaces provided.

A Short Questionnaire About Clubs and Societies

Your partner's name: _____

1. What do you know about the students' clubs and societies in your university?
   _____

2. What's the approximate number of clubs and societies here?
   _____

3. Can you give the names of some of these clubs and societies?
   _____

4. Are you a member of any of them?
   _____

5. Which of them do you know a lot about?
   _____

(Continued)

6. Which of them would you most want to join?
   _____

7. What are your hopes and expectations about the students' clubs or societies in your university?
   _____

Task b You will hear someone introducing the sports center of a university. Listen to the recording and complete the missing information in the chart below.

Notes About the Sports Center

Membership fee: _____
Where to register: _____
Time to register: _____
What to bring for registration: _____
Opening hours: _____
Hours for 50 percent discount: _____
Facility 1: _____
For which sports: _____
Facility 2: _____
For which sports: _____
Other facilities and arrangement: _____

Task c Pair-work: Below is a questionnaire about time. Interview each other with this questionnaire and record your partner's answers in the spaces provided after each question.

Questionnaire

Customs and Attitudes About Time

1. You invite friends to dinner at your place and plan on eating at 9 p.m.
   a. At what time would you ask people to come?
   _____

UNIT 7 Clubs/Societies

(Continued)

    b. How would you feel if someone comes at 10: 00?

2. In your place, you are invited to a dinner party for 9: 00.
    a. At what time would you probably arrive?

    b. Why?

3. You are invited to a big dance in your place that begins at 9: 00.
    a. At what time would you probably arrive?

    b. Why?

4. In your place, a friend has promised to meet you at a local coffee shop at 9: 00, but he isn't there when you arrive.
    a. If he doesn't show up, at what time would you give up and leave?

    b. How would you feel about your friend being half an hour late?

5. You have promised to pick up your sister at 9: 00 a.m. to go shopping, but you run into problems and arrive late.
    a. After what time would you feel like you have to say you are sorry for being late?

    b. What would you say?

6. You have a dentist's appointment at 9: 00 a.m.
    a. At what time would you probably arrive?

    b. What would happen if you arrive late?

    c. In your place, do dentists schedule appointments for specific times?

7. You have a job interview at 9: 00 a.m. in your place.
    a. At what time would you probably arrive?

(Continued)

> b. What would happen if you arrive late?
> _____
>
> 8. Are your answers typical of the way most people from your place would respond?
> _____
>
> **Signature of partner:** _____
> **Place of birth:** _____

Group Projects

1. At the group meeting, exchange your undergraduate experiences of participating in your society activities, also discuss some of the students' clubs and societies in your present university. Talk about the benefits and problems of joining these clubs or societies and make any comment. Choose one of you as the representative of your group. This representative will have about five minutes to report to the whole class about the points you have made at the group meeting in the next class.

2. At the group meeting, choose a society you would like to start in the university. Work out the objectives, locations/times of meetings, membership fee, plans for future activities, etc. for your society. And then elect the president and/or department heads of the society. Make detailed plans for the group presentation about your society before the whole class. You can use power point files and/or other aids to help you. You may decide whether to choose one member (the president) or all members (e.g. president and department heads) to make the presentation.

Unit 8 Past Schooling

Listening One: Once upon a time

Task a Do you still remember what happened to you when you were still at primary school? Below is a questionnaire about one's childhood. Join a partner and interview each other with this questionnaire. Record your partner's answers in the spaces provided.

A Short Questionnaire to Discover Your Past Schooling	
Partner's name: _____	
1. What do you remember about your first holiday?	
2. What do you remember about your first day at school?	
3. Did you have a good time at school?	
4. Did you have a favorite teacher?	
5. Did you have a worst teacher?	
6. What do you remember about your last day at school?	

Task b You will hear Jack and Shirley answering these questions for a radio program. Take notes to complete the chart below as you listen to the recording.

Questions	Jack	Shirley
1.		
2.		
3.		

(Continued)

Questions	Jack	Shirley
4.		
5.		
6.		

> **Lexical items:**
>
> | | | |
> |---|---|---|
> | teddy | emblazon | to get my own back on someone |
> | chap | soak | bucket |
> | toast | Lake District | porridge |
> | incident | goody-goody | hymn (song) |

Task c **Pair-work:** What do you remember about your early schooldays? Do you have any interesting stories to tell your partner about any of these things?

- Your best memory at primary school
- Your worst memory at primary school
- Your last day at school
- The teachers who left you a deep impression
- The most important thing that happened to you
- Your greatest success at school
- Your greatest failure
- Something unfair that happened to you
- Your school buildings

Task d What do you remember about your college life? Some old friends are going to remember their days together in college. Listen to the recording and fill in the chart below.

The way they looked
Curtis: _____
Grace: _____
Martin: _____
Their worst memory: _____
_____
_____

UNIT 8 Past Schooling

(Continued)

The way they looked
Curtis: _____
Grace: _____
Martin: _____
Their best memory: _____   _____   _____
Last day of college: _____   _____   _____

Lexical items:

incredible	waist	jeans	was scared stiff
petrify	demonstration	scary	skip

Task e Pair-work: Join a partner and interview each other with the questions below. Record your partner's answers in the spaces provided.

Interview Questions:

1. What do you remember most about your college days?
   _____

2. What is your worst memory in college?
   _____

3. What was your best memory in college?
   _____

4. What did you do on the last day?
   _____

Listening Two: A good start

Task a You are going to hear three people talking about their schooldays. Answer the following questions by taking notes as you listen to the recording.

1. What did William do on his first day at school?
   _____

49

2. How did Brenda feel walking up the long avenue of trees?

   _____

3. Why did Angela's teachers want her to stop doing maths?

   _____

4. What does William think is the most important thing about education?

   _____

5. Why does Brenda think qualifications are so important?

   _____

Lexical items:		
vaguely	boarding school	uniform
uneasy	kid	forgive
unpopular	secondary school	avenue
satchel	alive	passionate
poke fun at somebody	geography	adore
horrible	Hugs-Bugs	gear

Task b Group-work: Work in small groups and find out from your partners as much as you can about their early childhood. For example:
- Birthday and other celebrations
- Life when they were in school
- Vocation experiences
- First train trip/drink/cigarette/interview, etc.

Task c Pair-work: Interview each other, using the following questionnaire. Record your partner's answers in the spaces provided.

Questionnaire
Your Family Life

1. Tell me your full name and how it was chosen.

   _____

2. When you were a child, who lived with you?

   _____

UNIT 8 Past Schooling

(Continued)

3. When you were a child, who took care of you when your parents were not home?

4. When you were growing up, what were your responsibilities in the house?

5. As you were growing up, how did your parents feel about you becoming independent?

6. What was family life like in your home when you were a teenager? What was it like when you disagreed with your parents?

7. In your culture, where do young adults live before they get married? Why?

8. In your culture, what do people think of a 27-year-old person who lives at home with his or her parents? Explain.

9. Nowadays, when you have a problem, who do you go to for help? Is that typical in your culture?

10. In your culture, where do older people live, and what money do they live on?

11. When does your whole family get together?

12. How do people in your extended family depend on each other or help each other out?

Signature of interview partner: _____
Place of birth: _____

Group Projects

1. At the group meeting, discuss with your group members your most impressive experiences in your primary school and university life. Choose one of you as the representative of your group. This representative will have about five minutes to report to the whole class about some interesting experiences you have described at the group meeting in the next class.

2. Begin alone. What was the worst day of your life—the day when everything seemed to go wrong? Try to remember the details and perhaps make a few notes. Or you may decide to invent a story with yourself as a hero or a heroine. But don't tell anyone if you are going to lie.

    At the group meeting tell your stories in turns. Describe afterwards who was telling the truth and who was lying.

    Work alone again and try to remember the best day of your life or invent a story of a happy day when everything went right.

    Again in groups, tell your stories and guess who was telling the truth.

    Choose a member from your group whose stories are the most interesting. The person should tell the whole class the stories in the next class.

Unit 9 Past and Future

Listening One: It's all in the past

 Task a

Do you know a lot about your family history? Have you heard some interesting stories about your parents or grandparents? You are going to hear four people talking about their family histories. As you listen, complete these sentences or answer the questions by taking notes.

1. Simon
   a. Simon's great grandfather came here _____.
   b. He met Simon's great grandmother after _____.
   c. In Russia, Simon's great grandmother's family _____.

2. Ronda
   a. How long has Ronda's family been living in Australia?

   b. Where had her family been living in England?

   c. Why did they decide to emigrate?

   d. When did Ronda's father meet her mother?

   e. What happened when he married her?

3. Alistair
   a. How far back can Alistair trace his family tree?

   b. Who built the house he now lives in?

c. Why did they decide to sell the family mansion?

d. He gave the mansion to the nation after

e. What's been happening since 1926–1927?

4. Caroline

   a. Where had Caroline's great grandmother been living?

   b. Where did she meet her husband?

   c. Caroline met Armand in the supermarket. What happened?

Lexical items:		
at the turn of the century	original	lad
Melbourne	ancestor	William the Conqueror
mansion	discomfort	gala ball
gorgeous		

Task b **Pair-work:** Do you have any interesting stories about your parents or grandparents? Has your family ever moved from one place to another? Try to prepare some short anecdotes to link your present with their past. Share these anecdotes with your partner.

Task c **Pair-work:** Do you have a family tree? Make a simple family tree for your family. Then, join a partner and describe your family tree to your partner.

My Family Tree

UNIT 9 Past and Future

Listening Two: A vision of the future

 Task a   You will hear a conversation about the science fiction movie *Soylent Green*. *Soylent Green* is about New York City in the year 2022. What do you think New York City will be like in 2022? Listen to the recording and either make choices or take notes to answer the questions below.

1. Which of the following are in short supply or no longer exist in 2022?

apartments	water	soybeans
soil	soap	fuel
lettuce	beef	ocean plants

2. What is the percentage of unemployment?

   | 20% | 30% | 50% | 70% |

3. What is the weather like?

   _____

4. What do people eat? What is it made of?

   _____

5. Which of the two speakers in the conversation is the more optimistic about the future?

   _____

   Lexical items:
crawl	awful	scene
running water	amazing	cracker
disgusting	greenhouse effect	

Task b   Pair-work: Work with a partner and ask each other the questions in this list. Be optimistic about the future, but don't invent an absurdly romantic fantasy. Talk about your hopes and expectations. Take brief notes of your partner's answers.

In 20 years' time:
1. How will your life be different from now?

   _____

2. Where will you be living?

   _____

3. What job will you be doing?

   _____

4. What will you do on a typical day?

   _____

5. How will you spend your spare time and holidays?

   _____

Task c **Pair-work:** Work with a partner and discuss the kind of life you would like and the kind of life you would dislike. Note down your partner's answers in the chart below.

	Like	Dislike
Job/Activity		
Family Situation		

Task d You will hear an interview with a biologist. Which of the following best describes what he talks about? Listen to the recording and make your choice by circling the corresponding letter.

a. A scientific experiment

b. The behavior of certain animals

c. Experiments on sick animals and human beings

d. Some scientific research and its possible future applications:

Lexical items:
plot   freeze   Cardiff
circumstance   terminal illness   administer
prolong   multiple sclerosis

Task e **Pair-work:** A time machine is believed to be a device which could take you back to the past or far ahead into the future. Imagine that you are going on a journey 50 years into the future. You only have enough room in your time machine for some of the equipment listed below, but not all. Put each item into one of these categories:

UNIT 9 Past and Future

1. Absolutely essential _____
2. Necessary _____
3. Useful but not absolutely necessary _____
4. Not really needed _____
5. No use at all _____

aspirins	cheque book
gun	bicycle
English phrase book	Russian dictionary
notebook	clock
sleeping bag	camera
compass	sunglasses
map of the world	pack of playing cards
television set	cash
raincoat	warm clothes

Group Projects

1. Look at the chart below. What are the good points and bad points with each of the four stages in one's life? Which time of life do you think is the best? Why do you think so? Have a discussion with your group members and write down the main points in the spaces provided. Choose one of you to make a presentation in the next class about the main points you make at the group meeting.

	Good Points	Bad Points
Childhood (below 18)		
Young adulthood (18–35)		
Middle age (35–50)		
Old age (above 50)		

(Continued)

2. First work alone. Write notes about some of the things you used to do when you were very young, and some things you didn't use to do. Try to think of things that are interesting or amusing. Also write down some things you hope and plan to do in the future. Now interview your group members about their lives and briefly record their answers. Choose one of you to make a presentation in the next class about the main points you make at the group meeting.

	Used to Do	**Didn't Use to Do**	**Hopes**	**Plans**
You				
Others				

Unit 10 Commercials/Advertisements

Listening One: Clensip

Task a Do you often watch TV programs? What do you think of the commercials on TV? What do you think of advertisements in newspapers? You will hear two advertisements. Listen to the recording and complete the information about the advertisements.

Lexical items:			
powdery flake	dandruff	itchy	scalp

	Name	Effect
Ad. 1		
Ad. 2		

Task b The Goodhayes Advertising Agency are developing the image for a new product with the name Clensip. This recording is about part of their committee meeting. Listen to the recording and complete as much of the required information as you can.

1. What is Clensip?

   _____

   _____

2. Ideas suggested for the advertising campaign:

   _____

   _____

3. Uses of Clensip:

   _____

   _____

4. Adjectives used to describe Clensip:

   _____   _____   _____

   _____   _____

> **Lexical items:**
>
> | | | | |
> |---|---|---|---|
> | campaign | packaging | can | competitor |
> | alternative | fattening | sailing boat | yacht |
> | refreshing | soothing | sparkling | bathe |

Task c **Pair-work:** Discuss with a partner and take notes about: advantages and disadvantages of commercials and advertisements; suggestions for improving the present advertising system; suggestions for how people can be made aware of the negative effects of commercials and advertisements.

Listening Two: Waverley—a holiday you'll never forget

Task a Anthony Morgan works for a small advertising agency. He specialises in video advertisements, and writes glowing descriptions of the hotels and holidays which are advertised in the videos. Today, however, he is far from, and so he goes to see his boss. Listen to their meeting and fill in the following form.

Employee Complaint	
Employee's name	Anthony Morgan
Position	Advertising copywriter
Subject of complaint	
Complaint	
Reasons given	
Result of meeting	

UNIT 10 **Commercials/Advertisements**

> **Lexical items:**
>
> glowing   a pack of lies   lumpy
> rating   Tourist Board   rotten

Task b Here is the script which Anthony brought to his boss. Listen to the recording and write down the missing words.

The Waverley Hotel welcomes you to some of the most beautiful countryside in the Southwest, and the service it offers 1) _____ . You stand at the elegant front door, and your 2) _____ is of comfort and welcome. You glance into one of the 3) _____ restaurants, and see that the menu is excellent, and the tablecloths and silver are 4) _____ . The standard of waiting is 5) _____ , and 6) _____ are everywhere.

Here you will come to sample the fish, freshly caught in the nearby stream, and 7) _____ . You may even enjoy the home-made pie, which is produced by the cook to a secret recipe. 8) _____ what the ingredients are. There are other Waverley specialities which you will 9) _____ . There is, for example, a long table of freshly-made desserts, creating a beautiful sight, and usually scent, 10) _____ .

You make your way to your room. 11) _____ you have one of the large, 12) _____ rooms at the front of the house, overlooking the gardens. Or perhaps you have chosen one of the smaller rooms, but you 13) _____ be comfortable in one of these. Remember, 14) _____ bed is more comfortable than a Waverley bed. You 15) _____ find the staff, who 16) _____ there to answer your questions, polite and courteous, and should you require anything at any time, such as 17) _____ sheets or a 18) _____ cup of tea, you are very welcome to 19) _____ .

20) _____ you stay at the Waverley you will have a holiday which you will never 21) _____ , and at a price which will 22) _____ !

Task c Look at the following translation of the advertisement. It is positive in every way. It is, in fact, the translation of only the written version of the advertisement. In the recording, the speaker deliberately stresses some words instead of others. As a result, the meaning of the advertisement becomes completely negative. Listen again and mark all the words that are stressed in the recording. Try to work out the real meaning of the advertisement.

欢迎阁下来西南部景色秀丽的乡村观光旅游，下榻威佛利饭店。您将受到我们的殷勤接待。百闻不如一见。来宾一到饭店漂亮的正门，舒适之感便会油然而生。瞧瞧饭店的两个餐馆：窗明几净，座无虚席；佳肴盈桌，清洁卫生。卓越的服务，上乘的标准，饭店服务人员随时恭候您的光临。

下榻威佛利饭店少不了要品尝这里的鱼鲜。鱼，是就近从小河中捕捞的，现宰现烹。您还可以尽情地享用饭店的家常馅饼——这可是威佛利的一绝，独家经营，配料保密。威佛利还有其他一些特色食品供您选择。别的且不论，单说那甜点就足以令人馋涎欲滴：热烘烘，香喷喷，口味齐，花色多，摆满了长长一大桌。

饭后步入您的房间。无论您住的是可以从中俯瞰重重花园的高档大房间，还是普通小客房，它们均同样令人舒适惬意。有道是，饭店床位千千万，下榻威佛利最舒坦。我们的服务员彬彬有礼，端茶送水，殷勤周到，清洗打扫，随叫随到，凭您安排吩咐，任您调遣使唤。

下榻威佛利饭店将使您度过一段终生难忘的假日，而饭店的低廉价格更会令人感到无比惊喜。

Task d **Pair-work:** Below is a questionnaire about money. Work with a partner and interview each other with this questionnaire. Record your partner's answers in the spaces provided.

Questionnaire About Money

Partner's name: _____

1. Imagine this situation: You suggest to a friend of the same sex, "Let's go out for lunch." When the check comes for the meal, who pays? Why? Is that the usual custom in your place?

   _____
   _____

2. Imagine this situation: You go out on a date to the movies with someone of the opposite sex. Who would you expect to pay for the evening? Why? Is that the usual custom in your place?

   _____
   _____

UNIT 10 Commercials/Advertisements

(Continued)

3. Imagine this: You borrow 2 yuan from a friend to make a phone call. The next time you see your friend, do you return the money? Why or why not? Would your friend accept it? Why or why not?
   _____
   _____

4. Imagine this: You need 200 yuan for an emergency. To whom would you go to borrow the money? Would you return it? What would happen if you did not pay it back?
   _____
   _____

5. Imagine this: The college that you want to attend costs 5,000 yuan more than you have. Where, or from whom, would you try to borrow the money? In China, when people are in this situation, what choices do people have?
   _____
   _____

6. Imagine this situation: the semester is ending, and you want to thank your favorite teacher for all her help. Would you buy her a pretty bracelet for 150 yuan to thank her? Why or why not? What would she think if you did?
   _____
   _____

7. In China, is it OK to ask friends how much money they make? Why or why not?
   _____
   _____

8. Is it OK to ask friends who paid for their car? Their house? If not, why not?
   _____
   _____

9. Do you think it is OK to ask these questions of someone you have just met, or an acquaintance? Explain.
   _____
   _____

10. How would you feel if a guest at your house asked you how much you paid for your stereo?
    _____
    _____

Signature of partner: _____

Group Projects

1. At your group meeting discuss the two speakers' (Anthony and his boss) attitudes in the conversation. Who is right and who is wrong? Give reasons to justify your argument if you take the boss' side or vice versa. Choose one of you to make a presentation in the next class about the main points you make at the group meeting.

2. Listen to the recording of Anthony's rewritten version of the advertisement as many times as possible. Work out the Chinese translation with your group members. You should read your group's translation before the whole class next time.

Unit 11 Entertainment

Listening One: Finding out what's going on in town

 Task a Do you often see films? What kind of films do you like? You are going to hear three people discussing what film they want to see tonight. Now listen to the recording. Fill in the missing information in the ads. Then complete the note to John. The names of the cinemas are Palace, Circle Theater, Metro, Westside Cinema.

The Empire Strikes Back Theater: _____ Times: _____ Ticket price: _____	*Casablanca* Theater: _____ Times: _____ Ticket price: _____
Rocky III Theater: _____ Times: _____ Ticket price: _____	*Kramer vs. Kramer* Theater: _____ Times: _____ Ticket price: _____

John

We're going to see _____ at _____ p.m. at the _____ Theater. Meet us at the Sunset Bar and Grill (across the street) at _____ p.m. or outside the theater at _____.

> **Lexical items:**
> Arts and Leisure Section   showtime   tear jerker
> Humphrey Bogart   Ingrid Bergman   Bar and Grill
> fan   figure out

65

Task b You will hear a conversation between a man and a woman. They are discussing which film they'd like to see. Listen to the recording and write down what they say about each of the films.

Films	Information
1. *Casablanca*	
2. *Rambo*	
3. *Psycho*	
4. *E.T.*	
5. *Chariots of Fire*	
6. *Godfather*	

Lexical items:
wartime	oldish	revolting
gratuitous	thriller	dated
gory	Brando	weepie

Task c Pair-work: Below is a short questionnaire about movies. Join a partner and interview each other with this questionnaire. Record your partner's answers in the spaces provided.

A Short Questionnaire About Your Preference of Movies

Partner's name: _____

How often do you watch a movie?

_____

What movies have you seen recently?

_____

What are they about?

_____

What do you think of them?

_____

UNIT 11 Entertainment

(Continued)

What movies have left you a very deep impression? Why?
_____

What movies do you dislike the most? Why?
_____

What movies would you most like to see? Why?
_____

What particular movies would you most want to suggest to our class? Why?
_____

Task d Pair-work: The following is a list of different types of films. With a partner, discuss each of these types. Arrange them in your order of preference. Justify your choices with your reasons.

Western	thriller	detective	musical
spy	action	documentary	science fiction
comedy	love	horror	adventure
war	cartoon	disaster	

Listening Two: This is nine o'clock news

Task a Pair-work: Do you often watch TV? What TV programs do you like best? What programs do you dislike most? Join a partner and ask each other these questions. Complete the chart below with your partner's answers.

TV Programs: My Choices	
Partner's name: _____	
Five TV programs I like best	Five TV programs I dislike most

Task b You will hear a TV announcer telling viewers about programs on her TV station tonight. Listen to the recording and complete the blanks in the newspaper excerpt below.

TV America International: Tonight's TV Programs

7:05   Regional Special
— Part of a documentary series on traditional ways of living in the USA— tonight the 1) _____ communities in Pennsylvania.

2) ____   The News

8:10   High Society
— Episode number 3) _____.

9:00   Variety Show
— A live 4) _____ _____ with Eric Clapton. Woody Allen and the rock 5) _____ "Fusion."

10:00   Cleaver the Cat
— 6) _____.

7) ____   Sports
— Today's national and international sporting events.

11:00   Late Night 8) _____

11:15   9) _____
— The health program—tonight on the dangers of keeping fit.

12:00   Tootsie
— Midnight 10) _____ with Dustin Hoffman.

Lexical items:

Dutch	Pennsylvania	episode
series	live show	highlight
Dustin Hoffman (an actor)		light-hearted

Task c Pair-work: Below is a questionnaire about a person's top ten favorites from China and from the rest of the world. Interview each other and complete the questionnaire by writing down your partner's answers. Give explanations and descriptions about some of your choices.

UNIT 11 Entertainment

Name: _____

Your Favorite	Chinese	International
TV show		
Actor		
Actress		
Movie (title)		
Book (title)		
Author		
Composer		
Singer		
Group or band		
Record		

Group Projects

1. At your group meeting discuss a few impressive movies that you have ever seen. First briefly describe the story lines, and then talk about the most impressive parts of the movies. You may suggest a few best movies for your group members to see. Choose one of you to make a presentation in the next class about the main points you make at the group meeting.

2. Before the group meeting, buy a weekend issue of an English newspaper. At the group meeting discuss the TV programs which will be shown in the coming week. What programs do you plan to watch? Why do you want to watch these programs? You can discuss these questions by referring to the Arts and Leisure Section of the newspaper. One of you should prepare to make a group presentation in the next class.

Unit 12 Climate and Weather

Listening One: Watching the weather

Task a Pair-work: Discuss with a partner and think of as many words, either nouns or adjectives, as you can that describe the climate and different weather conditions. One of you should write down these words. You are supposed to think of at least twenty words within five minutes. Examples of such words are: cold, rain, hot, etc.

_____

_____

_____

_____

Task b You will hear a weatherman giving the forecast on the TV evening news. The forecast is about the weather conditions in some cities in North America. Listen to the recording and write down the predicted weather conditions in these cities.

Chicago: _____ San Francisco: _____
Los Angeles: _____ Denver: _____
Dallas: _____ Toronto: _____
Montreal: _____ Miami: _____

Lexical items:		
scattered showers	outlook	thermometer
dip	freezing point	unseasonably

UNIT 12 Climate and Weather

Task c You will hear a weather forecast for Europe and the Mediterranean areas. Listen to the recording and write down the temperatures and weather conditions in these countries.

Britain: _____   Sweden: _____
France: _____   Spain: _____
Italy: _____   Greece: _____
Southern Mediterranean: _____   Switzerland: _____

Lexical items:	
Mediterranean	hazy
pressure	hit the headline
thunderstorm	Morocco
nightfall	Alps

Task d Pair-work: With a partner, discuss the climate in China during each of the four seasons. Note down what you say in the chart. Then choose the place you would prefer to live in because of the climate there.

	The Climate			
	Spring	Summer	Autumn	Winter
North China				
South China				

Listening Two: News about the weather

Task a You will hear another weather forecast for North America. Listen to the recording and write down the temperatures and weather conditions beside the cities on the map below.

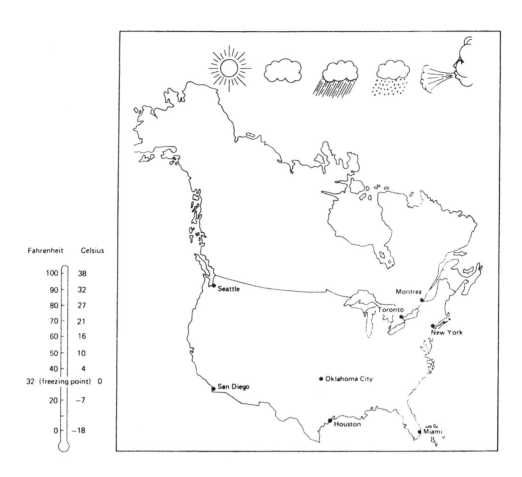

Lexical items:		
thermometer	flurry	update

Task b   **Group-work:** Work in groups of four or five. Decide together what advice you would give to a foreign visitor to your own city about the weather he or she might expect. One of you should take notes.
— Which is the best month to come here?
— Which is the most unpleasant month to come here?
— What kind of clothing would you recommend the visitor should bring if he or she comes from a country with a climate like that of Britain or from a country with a very hot climate?

Task c   **Pair-work:** With a partner, look at the following international weather report and locate the foreign cities on a world map.

UNIT 12 Climate and Weather

Foreign Cities
Weather and Temperatures Yesterday

City	High Temperature	Low Temperature	Weather
Amsterdam	82	70	clear
Athens	90	72	shower
Amsterdam	82	70	clear
Athens	90	72	shower
Bangkok	90	75	rain
Berlin	82	59	cloudy
Brussels	86	54	clear
Cairo	93	73	clear
Helsinki	75	50	cloudy
Jerusalem	88	72	clear
Johannesburg	59	28	clear
Moscow	66	48	rain
Nairobi	70	55	overcast
New York	70	54	clear
Oslo	80	64	clear
Seoul	86	77	shower
Stockholm	77	59	cloudy
Sydney	65	49	clear
Warsaw	79	59	rain

Group Projects

1. At the group meeting, you can take turns to describe the climate of your hometown in the four seasons. Choose one of you to make a presentation in the next class about the main points you make at the group meeting.

2. What was the worst weather you have ever experienced? What was the experience like? Answer these questions by giving details about the experience at the group meeting. One of you should prepare to make a group presentation in the next class.

Unit 13 Accommodation

Listening One: The inside story

Task a Pair-work: Where is your home? Is it a house or a flat (an apartment)? How many rooms do you have? What are those rooms? What items or pieces of furniture are there in each of the rooms? Refer to the picture of a two-bedroom flat below. Join a partner and make a list of the items or pieces of furniture in each room. You should at least write 10 items for each room.

The Usual Items in a ...			
Living Room	**Bedroom**	**Kitchen**	**Bathroom**

Task b You are going to hear a house agent showing a young couple around an apartment. Listen to the recording and write down all the information you hear about the apartment.

Rooms	Items

UNIT 13 Accommodation

Lexical items:		
fitted	bed-sitting room	fold-away double bed
mattress	novel	wardrobe
attire	curtain	roller blinds
tumble dryer	electric cooker	cubbyhole

Task C You will hear a conversation between Mrs. Hunt and a house agent. The agent is showing Mrs. Hunt around the house she wants to buy. The house they are talking about is a typical house for a middle class family in Britain. Listen to the recording and write down the information you hear about the house.

Rooms and Other Parts	Information
Hall	
East-facing room	
West-facing room	
Kitchen	
Garden	
Dining room	
Location of the house	
Staircase	
Bedrooms	
Single bedroom	
Bathroom	

Lexical items:		
entrance hall	telephone point	airy
power point	central heating	install
wallpaper	decoration	daffodil

(Continued)

built-in cupboard	sink unit	lawn
gardening	scheme	handy
reception room	double glazing	partition wall
soundproof	trombone	steep
invalid	stairway	dreadfully
landing	fence	blue tiles
blue bath	carpet	

Task d **Pair-work:** With a partner, discuss your own home. Describe your homes to each other and take notes on what your partner says. Your description should include the following information about your home. You can draw a sketch to help you make your description.

type of accommodation (e.g. house or flat/apartment?)
its location (e.g. which floor?)
different rooms (e.g. living room, bedroom, kitchen, bathroom, study, dining place, balcony?)
locations of the rooms
items in each of the rooms
locations of the items

A Sketch of Our Home

UNIT 13 Accommodation

Listening Two: This window here has a lovely view

Task a Pair-work: Have you ever stayed in a hotel? What was the experience like? Join a partner and discuss with each other about the hotels. Make a list of the facilities and services a good hotel should offer to its guests. Complete the chart below.

Hotel Facilities	Hotel Services

Task b You will hear a bellhop taking a hotel guest to her room. Listen to the recording and note down the information about:

Facilities/Services	Locations

Lexical items:

drape	directory	nightstand	lobby
boutique	newsstand	laundry	bell captain
airport limo	room service	revolving cocktail lounge	

Task c Pair-work: What was the best hotel you have ever stayed in? What was the worst hotel? What was your experience like? What kind of hotels do you expect to stay in the future? What kind of experience would you like to have? Join a partner and interview each other with these questions.

Group Projects

1. Work alone. Refer to a classified dictionary or a picture dictionary and work out a list of 300 words relating to accommodation. Your vocabulary list should be in both Chinese and English and include words about different rooms, items and furniture in each of the rooms, decorations and equipment, etc. Submit your vocabulary list as your written homework in the next class.

2. What kind of house do you expect to have in 20 years times? Work alone. First design the house by drawing a picture of it or downloading an existing picture from the Internet. Prepare a short description of the house with no less than 200 words. Your description may include its location, size, different rooms, decoration, items of furniture and equipment, etc. At the group meeting, describe your house to your group members. Find out whose house is the most attractive one. This person should prepare to make a description of his or her house in the next class. All of you should submit the picture of your future home and your written description as your homework.

Unit 14 Stay Well

Listening One: Doctor's orders

Task a Have you ever been ill? Have you ever been to the hospital? Work in pairs and discuss words that are used to describe health, illnesses and medicine. Try to think of as many such words, both nouns and adjectives, as you can and make a list of them. Add at least 15 words to each column.

Health	Illnesses	Medicine/Treatment
strong	cold	pill
overweight	running nose	operation

Task b You will hear some conversations that take place in a doctor's office. A family doctor is consulted by four patients. Listen to the recording and complete the chart below with the patients' problems and the doctor's advice.

Patients	Problems	Advice or Treatment
1.		
2.		
3.		
4.		

Lexical items:			
bending	strain	heavy lifting	advisable
bothering	trip over	wrist	swell
X-ray	packet	waste-paper basket	prescribe

Task c You will hear four short daily conversations. Listen to the recording. Write down what is wrong with each person and the advice he or she receives in the table below.

Patients	Problems	Advice
1.		
2.		
3.		
4.		

Lexical items:			
How are you doing?	brandy	salad	chili
ice cube	sore	spoonful	lemon

Task d Pair-work: Below is a list of people you are familiar with. What is each of their health like? Join a partner and find out each person's health situation from your partner and complete the chart.

Family Health Chart	
Partner's name: _____	
Grandfather on father's side	
Grandmother on father's side	
Grandfather on mother's side	
Grandmother on mother's side	
Father	
Mother	

UNIT 14 Stay Well

(Continued)

Aunt(s)	
Uncle(s)	
Myself	
Other important relation(s)	

Listening Two: A healthy life

Task a Pair-work: Below is a chart with information about illnesses. Join a partner. First look at the information that is given to you. Then discuss an experience of your illness. Fill in the chart with your information.

Name of Illness	Possible Symptoms	Possible Treatment
Flu	fever, chills, runny nose, sore throat	aspirin, nasal spray, cough suppressant, bed rest
Allergy	sneezing, rash, runny nose, itchy swollen eyes	antihistamines, injections, change diet
Measles	red spots all over body, itching, fever	bed rest, keep patient away from other people
Asthma	breathing is difficult and has a wheezing sound	inhalers, living in area with warm, dry weather
Heart Trouble	shortness of breath, chest pain, nausea	easier living, medicine, surgery
(My problem)		

Task b You will hear three short dialogues about illnesses. For each of them, take notes about the symptoms and treatments. Then, write down the name of the illness that you think the people in the dialogue have.

Patients	Major Symptoms	Treatments	Possible Illness
1.			
2.			
3.			

81

Task c **Pair-work:** Below is a list of questions about food and exercises. Join a partner and interview each other with these questions. Note down your partner's answers in the spaces provided.

Questions:

1. What kind of food do you usually have?
   _____

2. What kind of exercises do you usually take?
   _____

3. What kind of food do you think you should have more?
   _____

4. What kind of food do you think you should have less?
   _____

5. What kind of exercises do you think you should take more?
   _____

6. What kind of exercises do you think you should avoid?
   _____

Task d Dr. Martin Answay writes a column in a popular women's magazine on health problems. He is also an expert on heart disease. Listen to an interview with Dr. Answay and write down what he says about keeping healthy.

Dr. Answay's suggestions:

1. Food you should have more:
   _____
   _____

   Food you should have less:
   _____
   _____

2. Exercise you should take more:
   _____
   _____

   Exercise you should take less:
   _____
   _____

UNIT 14 Stay Well

Lexical items:		
supposedly	full-fat milk	cheese
excessive	overproduction	cholesterol
liver	artery	stroke
insulate	cell membranes	hormone
animal fat	pasta	vigorous
twisting	brisk walking	sustained

Task e Pair-work: Join a partner and discuss the following issues.

1) Describe some habits which you think are healthy. Explain why.
2) Now describe some habits you consider unhealthy. Again, give your reasons.
3) Which of these famous quotations would you agree with? Are there any you would disagree with? Why?

— "I rarely walk anywhere, and when I do it is only to attend the funerals of those friends of mine who practise such dangerous habits." (Lord Curzon)

— "Smoking is the easiest habit in the world to give up. I know. I've done it. Hundreds of times!" (James Sydney Melbourne)

— "All you need in life is good health, a bit of luck and a sense of humor. The rest is easy." (Clark Gable)

Group Projects

1. Work alone. Refer to a classified dictionary or a picture dictionary and work out a list of 300 words relating to health, illnesses and medicine/treatment. Your vocabulary list should be in both Chinese and English and include words which are commonly used in people's daily lives. Submit your vocabulary list as your written homework in the next class.

2. At your group meeting find out from each other any problems you have concerning your health and give each other some suggestions to remedy the problems. Choose one of you to make a presentation in the next class about the main points you make at the group meeting.

Unit 15 What's My Line?

Listening One: Willing to train

Task a Below is a job-interview form. When you go to a Careers Advisory Office for advice about a job, you will usually be asked questions about the areas listed in the form. Read the form and fill it in with information about yourself.

Interview Form

Age: ☐ under 20   ☐ 20-30   ☐ 30-40   ☐ 40-50   ☐ 50-60
☐ over 60

Qualifications: ☐ school qualifications   ☐ college/university qualifications
☐ specific qualifications or skills

Interests: ☐ people   ☐ music   ☐ arts   ☐ crafts   ☐ animals
☐ travel   ☐ others

Personality: ☐ withdrawn   ☐ quiet   ☐ friendly   ☐ outgoing
☐ aggressive

Organisational ability: ☐ disorganized   ☐ careless   ☐ capable
☐ efficient   ☐ bossy

Intelligence: ☐ very slow   ☐ slow   ☐ average   ☐ bright
☐ exceptional

Attitude to work: ☐ apathetic   ☐ lazy   ☐ interested   ☐ diligent
☐ hard-working

Appearance: ☐ untidy   ☐ tidy   ☐ smart   ☐ elegant

UNIT 15 What's My Line?

🎧 **Task b** Catherine has just left school and she wants to find a job. She and her mother have come to speak to the Careers Advisory Officer. Listen to their conversation and write down the following information (if any) about Catherine.

Age: _____

Qualifications: _____

Interests: _____

Personality: _____

Organisational ability: _____

Intelligence: _____

Attitude to work: _____

Appearance: _____

Lexical items:		
Careers Advisory Office	Mind you	vet
brilliant	over-optimistic	overpower
the School Choir	hairdresser	

Task c **Pair-work:** Suppose you are at a job interview. One of you is the Careers Advisory Officer and the other wants to find a job. The Careers Advisory Officer should find out the following about the applicant by asking some questions. The applicant should answer the questions. The Officer should also record below the information given by the applicant. Change roles when this has been done.

Name: _____

Age: _____

Qualifications: _____

Interests: _____

Personality: _____

Organisational ability: _____

Intelligence: _____

Attitude to work: _____

🎧 **Task d** You will hear part of the two job interviews for an IT position. First read the questions for this interview. And then, listen to the recording and complete the chart below with what you hear. Notice that the last question for each applicant is different.

> **Lexical items:**
> salary and extras   on top of   pension scheme

Questions for the interview:
1. Why do you want to work for us?
2. What are your strengths and weaknesses?
3. Why do you think you'd be good at this job?
4. Where do you want to be in five years' time?
5. How much do you earn in your present job?
6. Is it possible to work flexible time or overtime?

Questions	Applicant One	Applicant Two
1.		
2.		
3.		
4.		
5.		

Task e Pair-work: Below is the questionnaire used for the job interview above. Suppose you are at a job interview for one of your ideal jobs, what are your answers to these questions? Join a partner and interview each other with this questionnaire.

> **Useful Questions for Job Interviews**
>
> **Partner's name:** _____
>
> Why do you want to work for us?
>
> _____
>
> What are your strengths and weaknesses?
>
> _____

UNIT 15 What's My Line?

(Continued)

Why do you think you'd be good at this job?
___

Where do you want to be in five years' time?
___

How much do you earn in your present job?
___

Is it possible to work flexible time or overtime?
___

Listening Two: What do you do?

 Task a   You are going to hear four people talking about their jobs. Before you listen, discuss in pairs what each of their jobs is like. As you listen, fill in the missing information.

Speaker A
His job: waiter in a bar
What he enjoys: ___
What he dislikes: ___

Speaker B
Her job: dance teacher
What she enjoys: ___
What she dislikes: ___

Speaker C
His job: artist
What he enjoys: ___
What he dislikes: ___

Speaker D
Her job: accountant
What she enjoys : ___
What she dislikes: ___

Lexical items:

stump (confuse)	blare
Ramos gin fizz (a drink)	pinball machine
Beatles (a famous band)	gratifying
conception	payroll

 Task b You are going to hear a conversation involving two people with the same name. The information about one of them is already given below. Listen to the recording and complete the information about the other person.

Information Card

Name: J.V. Brown   Female

Age: 21

Occupation: Model and beauty queen

Description: Tall (6 feet) with red hair and green eyes

Possible jobs: Modelling clothes

　　　　　　　Photographic model

　　　　　　　T.V. Advertisements

Information Card

Name: J.V. Brown   Male

Age: _____

Occupation: _____

Description: _____

Possible jobs: _____

Lexical items:

bracelet	jewellery	shortish
bald	plumber	astonishing

UNIT 15 What's My Line?

Task c Pair-work: What aspects of a job would give you the most satisfaction? Discuss with a partner and arrange the following in your order of preference. And then each of you should decide on a job which meets your requirements.

high salary	meeting people
helping others	variety in work
responsibility	security
social status	challenge
being your own boss	opportunity to travel
company name	city or place
self development	good pension scheme
accommodation	working conditions

Task d Pair-work: Below is a list of different jobs. Put them in the order in which they are regarded and paid in this society. Then arrange them in the order you think they should be regarded and paid.

school teacher	university professor
policeman	taxi driver
doctor	politician
nurse	lawyer
business person	actor
singer	engineer
secretary	journalist
shop-assistant	hair-dresser
farmer	soldier

Task e Pair-work: With your partner, take turns interviewing each other, using the following questionnaire. Make a few notes about each answer.

Questionnaire

Jobs—Past, Present, and Future

1. What kind of jobs (or part-time jobs) have you had?

   _____

(Continued)

2. What kind of jobs (or part-time jobs) do you have now? (Note: If your partner has never had a job, skip questions 3–8, and begin with question 9.)
   _____

3. What are (were) your responsibilities?
   _____

4. What is (was) a typical working day like for you?
   _____

5. Could you describe a typical week?
   _____

6. What do (did) you like most about the job?
   _____

7. What would you change about the job if you could?
   _____

8. How did you get the job?
   _____

9. What kind of jobs do you see yourself doing in five years?
   _____

10. How did you decide to go into this field?
    _____

11. What will you need to do to achieve your career goals?
    _____

12. What difficulties do you think might come up for you?
    _____

13. How are you planning to deal with them?
    _____

14. How does your studies help you with your career plans?
    _____

Signature of interview partner: _____

Group Projects

1. At the group meeting, discuss the job factors you think that are most important and describe your job expectations with each other. Choose one of you as the representative of your group. This representative will have about five minutes to report to the whole class about the points you have made at the group meeting in the next class.

2. Organize a job interview in which each of you take turns to play the role of a candidate and the rest of you act as the interviewers. Role play the job interview among your group members. Choose one interview from your group to role play it before the whole class next time.

Unit 16   Making Your Point

Listening One: Right or wrong?

Task a   Pair-work: What do you think of corporal punishment? Did you use to be spanked when you were a child? Join a partner and discuss these questions. Make your point about corporal punishment. Write down your opinions in the boxes. You could refer to the points provided. Add more points of your own.

Arguments in Favor of Spanking	Arguments Against Spanking

1. Spanking teaches the difference between right and wrong.
2. Spanking teaches fear rather than respect.
3. Problems should be solved without violence.
4. Spanking makes children listen.
5. Spanking leads to more violent behavior.
6. Children who are spanked spank their own kids later in life.
7. Other forms of discipline are more effective.
8. Spanking can be effective when done in a loving home.

Task b   You will hear a panel discussion on the long-term effects of corporal punishment. Three experts are going to tell us their opinions about spanking children. Listen to the recording and complete the chart below.

UNIT 16 Making Your Point

Expert	Opinion	Reason
Donald Sterling		
Phyllis Jones		
Lois Goldin		

 Nowadays people use the Internet a great deal in their daily lives. What do you think are important in using the Internet? You will hear a short lecture about the right and wrong on the Net. Listen to the recording and complete the notes below about the lecture.

Lecture Notes

Lecture Topic: _____

Definition of an ethical action:
_____

The goal of Computer Ethics Institute:
_____

1 Commandment:
_____

2 Commandment:
_____

3 Commandment:
_____

4 Commandment:
_____

5 Commandment:
_____

6 Commandment:
_____

7 Commandment:
_____

8 Commandment:
_____

(Continued)

9 Commandment:
10 Commandment:

Task d **Pair-work:** With a partner, discuss the following topics. What points would you like to make on each of them?
1. Job allocation system for college graduates
2. Price of food and service in college cafeterias
3. Examination requirements for college students
4. Policy of Chinese students going abroad
5. Allowance of undergraduates and graduates
6. Length of undergraduate and graduate studies

Listening Two: There's nothing I can do!

Task a You are going to hear three short conversations which take place in different situations. Listen to the recording and complete the information below.

	Speakers	One Person's Problem	The Other's Arguments
1.	A: _____ B: _____		
2.	A: _____ B: _____		
3.	A: _____ B: _____		

Lexical items:

sales slip (receipt)	warranty	expire
defective	bend the rule a bit	add insult to injury
nag	crumb	

UNIT 16 Making Your Point

Task b Are you for or against capital punishment? What arguments can you give for your position? You will hear two friends arguing about capital punishment. They have different opinions about it. Listen to the recording and write down the reasons the two of them give to explain their positions.

Reasons for capital punishment:
_____
_____

Reasons against capital punishment:
_____
_____

> **Lexical items:**
> execute   death penalty   deterrent
> crackerjack   judicial system   rehabilitation
> discrimination

Task c **Pair-work:** Look at the following list. Which of the problems are your problems? With a partner, discuss these problems and ask for and give suggestions to each other.
1. Too busy with the lessons
2. Worrying about examinations
3. No social life
4. Difficulties in finding a boy/girlfriend
5. No income
6. Worrying about the future
7. Not having enough money to buy things
8. Poor study/living conditions
9. Not having enough sports facilities

Task d A Simulation
Situation: A famous university is planning to have a salary reform. Apart from the salary offered by the state, the university plans to establish a new component of the salary for its staff members. This new component is called "salary of the university" and it comes out of the original bonus

of the staff members. Traditionally, this bonus has always been equally divided among the staff members, whether one is an assistant teacher or a professor. The point of the reform is to widen the difference of this amount according to each staff member's position in the university. As a result, an old professor might receive as much as four times the amount offered to an assistant teacher. And this old professor will be able to keep this part of the salary even after his retirement.

The university is now having a meeting at which both young and old teachers are invited to discuss this salary reform. Suppose you are a young teacher in the university. What points can you make to oppose this reform? If you were an old man who is about to retire, what points will you make to support the reform?

Group Projects

1. At the group meeting discuss five top social problems in China. What point can you make about each of these problems. You may have different viewpoints but you need to justify your answers with some supporting facts. Choose one of you to make a presentation in the next class about the main points you make at the group meeting.

2. At the group meeting you can also talk about five problems that are facing college students in China. What kind of solutions can you suggest for each of these problems? You may have different viewpoints but you need to justify your answers with some supporting facts. One of you should get ready to make a presentation in the next class about the main points you have come out at the group meeting.

Unit 17 Sports

Listening One: Which sport?

Task a   **Pair-work:** Do you like sports? Do you often do some sort of physical exercise? Work in pairs and think of as many words as you can which are related to or describe sports. Make a list of these words in the spaces provided. Add at least 15 words to each column.

Sports Names	People Involved in Sports	Sports Places and Tools
running	coach	swimming pool
cycling	athlete	shuttle cocks

Here are the ten most popular sports in Britain and the USA for your reference.

Britain	**USA**
Association football	American football
Athletics	Field and track
Bowls	Baseball
Boxing	Basketball
Cricket	Boxing
Golf	Golf
Rugby	Ice hockey
Squash	Skiing
Tennis	Tennis
Snooker	Ten-pin bowling

🎧 **Task b**   You are going to hear some people talking about different physical exercises which help them keep fit. Which form of exercise is each of them talking about? Listen to the recording and note down the answers in the spaces provided.

Names	Forms of Exercises
1. Alison	
2. Susanna	
3. Tim	
4. Iain	
5. Bridget	
6. Deborah	

Lexical items:

aerobics	yoga	jolly
flabby	predominantly	sedentary
revive	reheel	Waterloo Rail Station

Task c   **Pair-work:** Below is a list of questions concerning sports. Join a partner and interview each other with these questions. Write down your answers in the spaces provided.

1. Which are the top ten popular sports in China?

2. What kinds of sports do you like to do?

3. How often do you take these exercises?

4. What sports would you most like to do? Why?

5. What sports do you least like to do? Why?

6. What sports do you most like to watch? Why?

UNIT 17 Sports

Listening Two: Sport and violence

Task a Do you like watching boxing? What do you think of it? You are going to hear three people giving their opinions about boxing. What does each of them think of it? Listen to the recording and record the answers briefly in the spaces provided.

Speakers	Opinions
1.	
2.	
3.	

Task b You will hear some people talking about a sport. Listen to the conversation and note down the answers to the questions below.

1. Which sport is being discussed?

2. Where do you think the people are?

3. How old do you think Steve is?

4. Is the atmosphere calm or tense?

5. What does each of the five people in the conversation think about the sport? Does each of them approve or disapprove of it? Fill in the table with what you hear.

Speakers	Approves of It	Disapproves of It	Opinions
Steve			
His father			
His mother			
His sister Laura			
His uncle John			

Lexical items:		
crisp	take a deep breath	parachute jump

 Task c You will hear a short talk about extreme sports. Listen to the recording and fill in the missing information in the chart.

Notes About the Talk:

The passage is about people called _____

These people like: _____ ;

_____ ;

_____ ;

_____ ;

_____ .

Task d Pair/Group-work: Discussion

1. Describe your favorite sport or game and explain why you enjoy it.
2. "Playing is a waste of time"—give your opinions about this statement.
3. Describe one of the popular sports you know of in Britain or the USA to your partners.

Group Projects

1. Work alone. Refer to a classified dictionary or a picture dictionary and work out a list of 300 words relating to sports. Your vocabulary list should be in both Chinese and English and include words which are commonly used in people's daily lives. Submit your vocabulary list as your written homework in the next class.

2. At your group meeting find out from each other five favorite sports and five least favorite sports of your own. You need to justify your answers with some supporting points. One of you should get ready to make a presentation in the next class about the main points you have come out at the group meeting.

Unit 18 Going on Holiday

Listening One: Holidays in the United States

Task a If you went on a four-week holiday to the United States what places would you want to go and what would you like to do there? Write five places and the things you would do in each place in the blanks below.

1. _____
2. _____
3. _____
4. _____
5. _____

Compare your answers in pairs and justify your answers.

Task b Sandra and John have just been to the United States on holiday. The following is a list of the places they have been to and the things they have done there. Listen to the recording and decide exactly who did what and who went where. Write Sandra (S) or John (J) after each place or thing.

Activities		Places	
Visiting my cousins	_____	California	_____
Visiting friends	_____	New York	_____
Camping	_____	Washington	_____
Visiting museums	_____	Boston	_____
Sailing	_____	Great Lakes	_____
Going to rock concerts	_____	New Orleans	_____

(Continued)

Activities	Places
Surfing _____	Disney world _____
Windsurfing _____	Youth Hostel _____
Eating hamburgers _____	
Eating hot dogs _____	
Visiting the Empire State Building _____	

Task C When you go to another country, you will probably want to travel around the place. Now listen to a customer talking with a travel agent. Fill in the missing information below. Which travel plan do you think is best for him?

Weekend Special
Fare: _____
Leaves Detroit on _____ at _____
Arrives in Miami at _____
Leaves Miami on _____ at _____
Arrives in Detroit at _____

7-Day Excursion
Fare: _____
Leaves Detroit on _____ at _____
Arrives in Miami at _____
Leaves Miami on _____ at _____
Arrives in Detroit at _____

Night Flight
Fare: _____
Leaves Detroit on _____ at _____
Arrives in Miami at _____
Leaves Miami on _____ at _____
Arrives in Detroit at _____

UNIT 18 Going on Holiday

> **Lexical items:**
> How are things going?   round trip   excursion
> red-eye   car rental

 Pair-work: With a partner, discuss the places you would like to visit. Suppose you had a holiday in which you could visit five different places in China or other countries. What would these places be? Tell each other why you want to visit these places and what you would like to do in each of these places.

Listening Two: Amazing journey

Task a Stephen Taylor is a famous canoeist. He has just returned to England after an amazing journey in his canoe. Listen to the interview with him by a radio reporter and complete the chart below with the relevant information you hear from the conversation.

Time	What Happened?	Conditions on River
Day one		
Day two		
Day three		
Days four and five		

> **Lexical items:**
> canoe   canoeist   block of ice
> rockface   waterfall

 You will hear the International Tourist Service program on Radio Europe International. The program is about what's on where in the five European countries: Holland, Switzerland, Germany, France and Belgium. Listen to the recording and match the names of the cities with the events in each of them.

Activities	Places
a. Impressionist exhibition b. Yachting regatta c. Picasso exhibition d. Canoeing events e. Exhibition of German food f. Bruce Sringsteen concert g. Beethoven's Fifth Symphony h. Traditional games and dancing i. International Athletics Championships	1. Amsterdam 2. Paris 3. Brussels 4. Stuttgart 5. Geneva 6. Weisbaden 7. Rotterdam

Lexical items:

folklore   regatta   orchestra   Rhine (a river)

Task c **Pair-work:** Hiking is a very popular hobby for many people to spend their weekends or holidays. What do you think of this hobby? Would you like to join in a team to hike a beautiful mountain some day? What ten most important precautions do you have to take before and during such a hike? Join a partner and discuss these questions. Take notes of your answers.

Precautions for a Hiking Holiday

1. _____
2. _____
3. _____
4. _____
5. _____
6. _____
7. _____
8. _____
9. _____
10. _____

Task d You will hear an expert giving advice about the ten most important precautions before and during a hiking holiday. Listen to the recording

UNIT 18 Going on Holiday

and take notes to complete the chart below.

Lexical items:		
first-aid kit	rations	sneakers

Precautions for a Hiking Holiday

1. _____
2. _____
3. _____
4. _____
5. _____
6. _____
7. _____
8. _____
9. _____
10. _____

Task e Pair-work: Tell your partner what your idea of a great summer vacation is. Look at the following suggestions for places and activities, and add others of your own.

Places
the mountains
the beach
a big city
a small town
a resort
the jungle
a village
an out-of-the-way hotel or resort
Other: _____
_____
_____

Activities

eating local food

sports—walking, bicycling, boating, swimming, sailing, water skiing, hiking, tennis, volleyball, golf

shopping

sightseeing—museums, historic monuments and buildings, natural wonders

relaxing—lying on the beach, reading

socializing—dancing, going to nightclubs and restaurants, visiting friends

camping—fishing, hunting

taking photos

doing nothing

Other: _____

_____

_____

Group Projects

1. At your group meeting discuss what kind of holiday you would expect to have in 20 years. Make a detailed plan about this holiday that should include your destinations, activities, living and traveling arrangement, etc. Decide whose plan is the most attractive. The person should get ready to make a presentation about your group work in the next class.

2. At the group meeting tell each other about your holiday experience. What was the best holiday you ever had? What made it so enjoyable? What was the worst one? Why was it so awful? Decide whose story is the most impressive. This person should prepare to tell his/her story to the whole class next time.

Listening Test 1

Section One

Directions: Below are Professor Hunt Williams' notes for the announcements he has to make at the final plenary session of an international conference on urban planning. Listen to his announcements and fill in the missing information.

1. Final discussion of urban pollution will move to Room _____.
2. Domestic shelter session will move to Room _____.
3. Return _____ to the Porter's Lodge.
4. Return discussion _____ to the session chairpeople by _____.
5. First coach for airport outside Kennedy Building at _____.
6. Second coach at _____. Delegates to arrive at least _____ before departure.
7. Drs Schapsinger, Garbeldi and Surinander: collect reprints from the _____.
8. Dr. Goldman (Chicago Institute) 6th Annual Convention of P.E.S., in Hawaii, in _____. Interested parties leave _____ at conference desk.

Section Two

Directions: You will hear an interview between a local newspaper reporter and Mr. Gibbon, whose hobby is stamp collecting. Mr. Gibbon is being asked a number of questions about his hobby. While you are listening to the interview, write some notes in the spaces in the reporter's notebook below.

Mr. Gibbon's Hobby: Stamp Collection

1. Age when he started collecting: _____
2. Number of years collecting: _____

3. First stamps: _____

4. Size of stamp collection: _____

5. Value of stamps: _____

6. Oldest stamp: _____

7. Countries collected: _____

8. Themes/subjects collected: _____

Sections Three

Directions: A man phones a building superintendent for information about an apartment for rent. Fill in the answers to his questions on the checklist.

Call About Apartment in Gazette

1. No. of bedrooms: _____

2. Rent: _____

3. Includes heat and electricity? _____

4. Average cost of utilities: _____

5. Washers/dryers in building? _____

6. Quiet building? _____

7. What floor? _____

8. Elevator? _____

9. Address: _____ Turner Drive

10. Near shopping? _____

11. Who to see: _____, # _____

12. Time: _____

13. Other information: _____

Listening Test 2

Section One

Directions: In this section you will hear an interview with a computer hacker. Listen to the recording and write down the hacker's answers to the questions below. You only need to give a short answer to each question. You will hear the recording once only. You now have 30 seconds to read the questions first.

Questionnaire for Interview with a Hacker

1. What name do you use as a hacker?

2. What kind of people do you target?

3. What do you do when you've hacked into someone's computer?

4. Why do you do it?

5. How do you feel when you're hacking into someone else's computer?

6. How much time do you spend hacking?

7. Are you part of a group or do you work alone?

8. What do you do with the stuff you download from other people's computers?

9. Can you tell us about any of your hacking jobs?

Section Two

Directions: In this section you will hear the director of a charity, the National Asthma Campaign (NAC), welcoming participants and introducing speakers at an Open Day. Complete the following sentences with no more than 3 words in each blank. You will hear the recording twice. You now have 30 seconds to read the incomplete sentences below.

1. The Open Day is held every _____.
2. Those attending can find out more about current _____.
3. The NAC spent _____ more on helping those with asthma than it did last year.
4. Only projects which have been vetted are considered for a _____.
5. People who have helped fight asthma ought to feel _____.
6. Lucy Wiggs's paper is about _____.
7. The second paper focuses on sufferers of _____, particularly those living in _____.

Section Three

Directions: In this section you will hear a lecture on world music. Listen to the recording and write down your answers to the questions below. You will hear the recording once only. You now have 30 seconds to read the questions.

1. In old times, long before recorded music, how did music spread from place to place?

2. In modern times, how does music spread all over the world?

3. What is one of the negative effects of the easily available recorded music?

4. What is one of the positive effects of recorded music?

5. What is World Music?

6. What is one example of World Music?

7. Why do some people think that World Music is a bad thing?

8. Why do some other people think World Music is exciting?

Oral Test

一、简介

本次口试采取一名考官和两名考生的方式进行。口试的目的是检查考生实际运用英语进行表达的能力。考生按顺序进考场后抽取一道题,在一旁按所抽题目要求准备 5 分钟,然后进行口试。与此同时,另一组考生进行准备。

口试分为两部分:

在第一部分,考官分别问考生 A 和考生 B 一至两个较为简单的问题(问题仅存考官手中),时间为 1 ~ 1.5 分钟。

第二部分由两个考生合作完成(任务由抽签决定),时间为 3.5 ~ 4 分钟。内容为:就某个话题发表自己的看法或完成某项模拟交际任务等。涉及的语言功能包括:就某个话题进行辩论、就某事采访某人、表达自己的见解、说服对方、提出建议等。

二、评分标准

口试满分为 25 分,15 分为及格线。考官根据考生的整体表现给出总分,分数一般在 12 ~ 22 分之间(12.5 = 50, 15 = 60, 17.5 = 70, 20 = 80, 22.5 = 90)。

90 分 (22.5)	发音准确,语调自然。语法正确,句型较复杂,词汇较丰富。发言流利,内容连贯。积极参与讨论,语言基本恰当。
80 分 (20)	
70 分 (17.5)	语音语调有缺陷,但不影响理解。句子结构较简单,词汇不够丰富。发言比较简短,内容不够连贯,但能完成任务。
60 分 (15)	
50 分 (12.5)	语音语调较差,妨碍理解。语法和词汇有较多错误。发言简短,内容不连贯。基本无法表达,无法完成任务。

三、注意事项

1. 为了防止替考，请考官要求考生出示带有照片的有效证件（学生证、身份证等）。登记后不必再问考生姓名直接进行口试的第一部分。

2. 每一道题只用一次。考官在考生完成交际任务后将题目收回，不再供考生抽取。

第一部分

考官从本部分试题中选一至两个问题分别提问考生 A 和考生 B（问题仅存考官手中），时间为 1 ~ 1.5 分钟。

Family life

1. Could you tell us something about your family?
2. What have you learned from your parents?
3. How different or similar are your parents?
4. Do you think you have a generation gap with your parents? Why or why not?
5. What do you think matters when choosing a spouse?
6. Why do people in China traditionally want to have a son?
7. Who does most of the cooking in your family?
8. What kind of parent do you intend to be?
9. What type of culture do you want your child to grow up in?
10. Are you going to bring your children up differently from the way you were brought up? Why?

Daily life

11. Some students skip their breakfast. Do you think it is a good idea?
12. Do you like Western food? Why or why not?
13. What do you normally do at the weekend?
14. Would you rather go shopping in a department store or in a supermarket? Why?
15. What do you usually do to keep fit?
16. Do you often read the newspapers?
17. Do you think watching TV is a waste of time?
18. What do you usually do with your friends?

English learning

19. How do you think you will use English in the future?
20. How do you usually practice English outside class?
21. What do you think is the best way to learn a foreign language?
22. Are you satisfied with your English learning? In what way? To what extent?
23. Do you think English can be learned in a short time? Why or why not?
24. What is your difficulty in learning English?
25. How much time do you spend learning English by yourself every week?

Campus life

26. What is your most impressive social activity on campus?
27. Do you think the students in Tsinghua have too much pressure? Why?
28. What do you usually do to reduce pressure or stress?
29. What do you like about Tsinghua University?
30. How do you think you will benefit from the education in Tsinghua University?
31. How do you make full use of the facilities on campus?
32. What role do you think the Internet plays in your life?
33. Can you list some of the annoying behaviors of Tsinghua students?
34. What changes has modern technology brought to your studies and work?
35. Have you ever been late for any class? How do you feel when you are late?
36. What advice will you give to those who are often late for class?
37. What's your attitude toward others' using mobile phones in class?
38. What do you think makes a good student?
39. What subject would you like to add to or take away from your curriculum and why?
40. What do you plan to do after graduating from Tsinghua University?
41. Where do you prefer to have self-study, in a classroom, the library or in your dormitory?
42. Where do you think students should live, on or off campus? Why do you think so?
43. Why did you choose Tsinghua University to pursue your master's degree?

Interests

44. Do you like music? What kind of music do you like best?
45. Do you think music is important in your life? In what ways?
46. What is your favorite sport and why?
47. What kind of movies do you like best? Who is your favorite movie star?
48. Which sportsman do you admire most? Why?

49. Can you tell me something about a book you read recently?

50. What color do you like? Why?

51. Do you like traveling and what places would you like to visit most?

Other topics

52. If you could change one thing about China, what would it be? Why?

53. If you got 10,000 yuan by chance or by luck, what would you do with that money?

54. How do you maintain friendship?

55. How do you usually spend your holidays?

56. What would you like to do when you visit a new city?

57. What do you think are the top 3 important inventions in the past 50 years?

58. What personal qualities do you like the most?

59. What personal qualities do you like the least?

60. What do you think is more important, money or fame?

第二部分

Pair-work tasks

1.

With the traffic problem getting worse, working at home as an option becomes a hot topic. Play the following roles, using specific reasons or examples to support your idea.

A: You think it is a good idea to work at home.

B. You don't think people can work well at home.

2.

With rapid economic development in China, travelling becomes popular for common people. Play the following roles, using specific reasons or examples to support your idea.

A: You think the best way to travel is a package tour.

B: You think the best way to travel is to explore everything by yourself.

3.

Generally speaking, people have to go through the process of dating before getting married. Play the following roles, using specific reasons or examples to support your idea.

A: You think it is important for people to date a lot before they get married.

B: You don't think people have to do so if they happen to fall in love at the first sight.

4.

It is said that famous athletes and entertainers earn millions of dollars every year. Play the following roles, using specific reasons or examples to support your idea.

A: You think these people deserve such high salaries.

B: You don't think these people deserve such high salaries.

5.

Internets have brought us problems as well as benefits. Play the following roles, using specific reasons or examples to support your idea.

A: You think Internet has more positive impact on our life.

B. You think Internets has more negative impact on our life.

6.

It is reported that a professor in Peking University claimed that higher education is now fostering competitive self-seekers, who give priority to individual benefit over everything else. Play the following roles, using specific reasons or examples to support your idea.

A: You agree with the professor's opinion.

B: You disagree with the professor's opinion.

7.

It is widely believed that many factors have influence on the formation of a person's character. Play the following roles, using specific reasons or examples to support your idea.

A: You think geographical position has great influence on a person's character.

B: You think family influence is greater than that of geographical location.

8.

In the age of multimedia, reading books is not as important as it once was. People can learn as much by surfing the Internet and watching television as they can by reading books. Play the following roles, using specific reasons or examples to support your idea.

A: I agree with the above statement.

B: I don't entirely agree with the above statement.

9.

It is known that parents often invest their own hopes and dreams in the younger generation. Discuss the following questions with your partner, using specific reasons and examples to support your idea.

Would you like your parents to pay much attention to you?

How do you feel when they do so?

What roles do you think parents should play?

10.

It was stipulated some years ago that plastic bags are not provided for free and very thin ones are banned altogether. Discuss the following questions with your partner, using specific reasons and examples to support your idea.

How well do you think this stipulation is enforced?

Do you refuse to use very thin plastic bags? What about people around you?

Why do you think it is difficult to ban the use of thin plastic bags?

11.

It is reported that the rate of sudden death has been growing among young and middle-aged white-collar workers. Discuss the following questions with your partner, using specific reasons and examples to support your idea.

What is your comment on this phenomenon?

What do you think is the cause?

What could people do to avoid such strategy?

12.

Some world-famous universities such as Harvard University and Cambridge University are offering free online courses to the public. Discuss the following questions with your partner, using specific reasons and examples to support your idea.

Have you ever heard of such courses and taken advantage of them?

What benefits do you think these courses bring to students?

What challenge do they present to teachers in China?

13.

Some young people believe that owning a home is closely related to their happiness. Discuss the following questions with your partner, using specific reasons and examples to support your idea.

Do you think home ownership is related to one's happiness?

Do you think people will really be happy when they take loans to buy an apartment in a big city?

What is your comment on living in lodgings?

14.

Every year there are people being injured or killed in traffic accidents. Discuss the following questions with your partner, using specific reasons and examples to support your idea.

What do you think are some possible causes for this problem?

What measures should be taken to prevent such tragedies?

15.

It is reported that a young thief broke into Mr. Li's apartment and fell dead in the process of stealing. His parents sued Mr. Li and asked for a compensation of 670,000 *yuan*. Discuss the following questions with your partner, using specific reasons and examples to support your idea.

What is your comment on this issue?

Should Mr. Li be asked to pay the thief's parents any money?

If you were the judge, what decision would you give?

16.

Teachers sometimes ask students to carry out group projects and give each member of the group the same score. Play the following roles, using specific reasons or examples to support your idea.

   A: You think it is appropriate to evaluate students in such a way.

   B: You think it is inappropriate to evaluate students in such a way.

17.

Different people have different ideas about a good job. Graduates are trying to find their dream jobs. Play the following roles, using specific reasons or examples to support your idea.

   A: You think being happy with a job is more important than having a high salary.

   B: You think having a high salary is more important than being happy with a job.

18.

It is reported that a student majoring in journalism wrote a letter to the president of the university, complaining that they have to study advanced math. Play the following roles, using specific reasons or examples to support your idea.

   A: You think it is a waste of time for students majoring in liberal arts to study advanced math.

   B: You think studying advanced math will do a lot of good even to students of liberal arts.

19.

It is said that China is going to levy house tax. Play the following roles, using specific reasons or examples to support your idea.

　　A: You think it is a good idea to levy house tax.

　　B: You think this will cause a lot of problems.

20.

Food safety is now a very serious problem in China and some measures must be taken to solve this problem. Play the following roles, using specific reasons or examples to support your idea.

　　A: You think moral education and financial penalty are essential to stop the problem.

　　B: You think only severe legal punishment is most effective to solve the problem.

21.

It is reported that an island for diserted babies was set up in front of the children's welfare institution in a Chinese city. Play the following roles, using specific reasons or examples to support your idea.

　　A: You are in favor of this practice.

　　B: You are against this practice.

22.

It seems that globalization is becoming a prevailing trend. Play the following roles, using specific reasons or examples to support your idea.

　　A: You think globalization has brought a lot of advantages and it's changing every aspect of our life.

　　B: You think globalization has presented great challenge to developing countries such as China.

23.

There are many dating programs on many Chinese TV channels. People appearing on such programs want to find their true love. Play the following roles, using specific reasons or examples to support your idea.

　　A: You think this is a good opportunity for singles to find their true love.

　　B: You think it is almost impossible for singles to find their true love in this way.

24.

It is generally agreed that there is a generation gap between parents and children.

Discuss the following questions with your partner, using specific reasons and examples to support your idea.

What words would you use to describe your parents' generation?

How would you characterize your own generation?

How is your generation portrayed in the media? Do you think this portrayal is accurate?

25.

It is reported that a couple has been in love for four years. Because the boy cannot afford to buy an apartment now, the girl chooses to marry their landlord, who is divorced without children. Discuss the following questions with your partner, using specific reasons and examples to support your idea.

If you were the girl, would you do the same? Why or why not?

Do you think true love still exists in modern society?

What do you think might be the cause for such a phenomenon?

26.

It is reported that an American student studying in Nanjing University bought two packets of French fries one day. He gave one to a beggar and sat together with her eating and talking. Discuss the following questions with your partner, using specific reasons and examples to support your idea.

If you were in the same situation as the American student, what would you do?

If you were the beggar, how would you feel? What insight can we get from this report?

27.

A Mayan prophecy goes that the Earth will come to an end some day in the near future. Discuss the following questions with your partner, using specific reasons and examples to support your idea.

Do you believe the prophecy will turn out to be true?

What challenges do you think the Earth is facing now?

What measures do you think we should take to make the Earth a safer place to live in?

28.

It is a common practice in universities for students to evaluate their teachers' work at the end of each term. Discuss the following questions with your partner, using specific reasons and examples to support your idea.

Do you think it is a good idea for teachers to be evaluated by students?

Do you value this opportunity of teaching evaluation?

What do you think might be some of its positive and negative sides?

29.

It is said that habit is the second nature. Discuss the following questions with your partner, using specific reasons and examples to support your idea.

Do you agree with the above statement?

Do you have any unhealthy habits?

What do you think we can do to form a good habit or get rid of a bad habit?

30.

Some people say it is their own business to spend money as they like. If they can afford they can enjoy any modern comforts and luxuries. Discuss the following questions with your partner, using specific reasons and examples to support your idea.

Do you agree with what these people say?

What effect do you think this type of living style may have on other people?

Do you think the government should impose heavy tax on luxury goods?

31.

It is reported that a graduate from a prestigious university applied to be a civil servant. He got the highest score for his written examination and job interview. But in the end he was refused employment for being an introvert (内向). Discuss the following questions with your partner, using specific reasons and examples to support your idea.

What is your comment on this phenomenon?

Do you think it is fair to base recruitment on personality?

What do you think students should learn from this incident?

32.

It is reported that an increasing number of students whose parents are officials are enrolled into key Chinese universities. Discuss the following questions with your partner, using specific reasons and examples to support your idea.

What is your comment on this fact?

Do you think it is fair for students from deprived families and less developed areas?

What do you think should be done to improve the situation?

Recording Script

Unit 1 Personal Information

Listening One

Task b

Alice Saunders is a young and attractive girl. She is a hotel receptionist. She works in a very good hotel in London, but she wants to change her job because she doesn't like the new manager. Every day he asks her "Will you go out with me tonight?" Every day she says "No!" So now here she is in the employment agency looking for a new job.

Clerk:	Good morning. Please take a seat.
Alice:	Thank you.
Clerk:	Now then. What's your name?
Alice:	Alice Saunders.
Clerk:	And what can we do for you?
Alice:	I want to change my job.
Clerk:	Uh-huh. And what do you do at the moment?
Alice:	I'm a hotel receptionist.
Clerk:	I see. OK. Well, let's write down a few details. What's your full name?
Alice:	Alice Mary Saunders.
Clerk:	Could you spell your surname for me, please?
Alice:	S-A-U-N-D-E-R-S.
Clerk:	And may I have your date of birth?
Alice:	The 7th of October, 1963.
Clerk:	Are you married or single?
Alice:	Single.

Clerk:	And may I have your address?
Alice:	9 Worthington Street, London, NW10.
Clerk:	I'm sorry, could you repeat that?
Alice:	9 Worthington Street, London, NW10.
Clerk:	And your telephone number?
Alice:	2744011.
Clerk:	Right. And ... what are you doing this evening?

Task d

Receptionist:	Good morning, can I help you?
Girl:	Good morning, I am interested in the English Lessons.
Receptionist:	Yes, er well we have two courses ... erm one is for three hours a day for four weeks and then we have another course which is more intensive... that's six hours a day for two weeks.
Girl:	Oh no, no, no, that's too many hours I want ... erm I want the three hours a day for four weeks.
Receptionist:	Three hours a day for four weeks. Good, erm ... could I have your name, please?
Girl:	My name is Isabel Martinez.
Receptionist:	Isabel Martinez. And how old are you?
Girl:	I am twenty-two.
Receptionist:	Twenty-two. Could I have your address, please?
Girl:	I'm staying in the Youth Hostel on High street.
Receptionist:	Youth Hostel, yes ... right. Would you want some accommodation? Do you want to stay somewhere else other than in the Youth Hostel?
Girl:	Well, that will depend on how expensive it is.
Receptionist:	Mm, hm. Well, the course and erm ... the accommodation with an English family which includes bed and breakfast and a packed lunch and an evening meal is 600 pounds.
Girl:	Oh, that's a lot of money. I don't think I can afford that ... (laugh)
Receptionist:	I'm sorry but it's very competitive with other courses (Erm). Other language schools offer the same sort of (Ahah) courses at the same sort of price.
Girl:	What, what do you offer me for that price ... apart from the bed and breakfast and the ...?
Receptionist:	We have a very good range of facilities. We've obviously very good

Recording Script

	teachers, well-trained teachers and very modern language-teaching facilities. And we also have TV and a video room, erm ... cookery and pottery classes, tennis courts if you like to play sport ... er ... a swimming pool ... er an excellent library, so the facilities are very good here.
Girl:	I see, when do the courses start please?
Receptionist:	The next course will be starting on Monday. That's this coming Monday which is ... er July the 15th.
Girl:	Right, erm, well yes, I'd like to take the course.
Receptionist:	Good, right. Now you just need to do an entrance test, just so that we can assess your ability, so that we know which class to put you into (Ah). Would you like to do that now?
Girl:	Yes, that would be lovely. Could I also ask you the ... er ... the money. Do I have to pay it all now or can I pay in ... in stages? I ... I don't have 600 pounds on me now.
Receptionist:	Ah, erm ... you, you'll have to pay a 20 pounds deposit now then (Yes) and pay the rest of the money on Monday morning before the ... the course starts (Ah ha) ... at er ten o'clock.
Girl:	Right and ...
Receptionist:	Can you do that?
Girl:	Yes, I can.
Receptionist:	Good, right so, erm ... I didn't get down which country you're from. Are you from Spain?
Girl:	Yes that's right. I'm Spanish.
Receptionist:	I thought so, yes and what do you do in Spain?
Girl:	I'm a student.
Receptionist:	Ah, right, good ... well, let's go along to the assessment room then and see how you get on.
Girl:	Thank you.

Listening Two

Task b

Terry:	Sure is hot out today.
Jean:	It really is. It might rain tonight, though.
Terry:	I hope so. Uh ... I've seen you around the office, but I don't think we've met.

	I'm Terry Moss. I work in the financial section.

Jean: Nice to meet you, Terry. I'm Jean Grant. I'm in the advertising department, up on seven.

Terry: The advertising section. Really? What do you do in advertising?

Jean: I'm a copywriter.

Commentator: A good way to start a conversation is to find something that you and the other person have in common. Here they talked about the weather. It affects them both. Second, they said their names. They introduced themselves. People often say their names after they've already started talking. Third, the man asked the woman about her job. Asking a question is a good way to move into a real conversation.

Task c

Number 1

A: You're new here, aren't you?

B: Yes, I just started this week.

A: I'm Ann Rogers.

B: I'm Sue Kelly.

A: It's nice to meet you, Sue.

B: Nice to meet you, too.

A: I was just going for my coffee break. Would you like to join me, Sue?

Commentator: Ann's strategy? Remembering names. She tries to remember the names of people she meets. Notice that she said, "It's nice to meet you, Sue." and "Would you like to join me, Sue?" The strategy: try to remember people's names by using them.

Number 2

A: Nice music, isn't it?

B: Yes. I really like jazz.

A: So do I. Especially Wynton Marsalis and Miles Davis.

B: I like them, too.

Commentator: This strategy is to add extra information. The woman didn't just say, "I like jazz, too." She said the names of two musicians she likes. It's really difficult to have a conversation with someone who just says "yes" or "no" or gives very short answers. Try to give extra information, especially when you're asked a question. Don't

Recording Script

just say "yes" or "no."

Number 3

A: Have you ever taken a class with this teacher before?

B: No, I haven't. But I've heard she's good.

A: I had her for a course last year. She's really good.

B: I'm glad to hear that. Oh, by the way, I'm Jan.

A: Nice to meet you. I'm Tony.

Commentator: The key here is to start a conversation by finding something you and the other person have in common—something that's the same, or that affects both of you. Here, the speakers are at school. They start by talking about the class and the teacher. At a party, you might mention the food or the music. What about other times? Anything that you and the speaker have in common—even the weather. You both already know it's cold or hot or rainy. But people talk about the weather because it's something they have in common. The strategy is to find something that is the same for you and the person you're talking to.

Number 4

A: Well, I'm a little shy. Of course I like meeting people, but it's kind of difficult. So before I meet someone, I sometimes think about what I want to say. I'll think of something about school or work. It depends where I am. Anyway, I usually do that before I say my name. So I guess planning what I want to say is important for me. I don't practice or memorize it or anything ... I just think about it.

Commentator: His strategy is to think about what he wants to say. By thinking about the topics, he knows what he wants to say—or at least what he wants to talk about. That makes it easier.

Unit 2   You and Me

Listening One

Task b

Interviewer: Excuse me ... er ... could I ask you a few questions?

First passer-by: Certainly, yes.

Interviewer:	Um ... pl ... could you tell me what you enjoy most in life?
First passer-by:	What I enjoy most in life? I think I enjoy ... um ... a nice meal.
Interviewer:	Mmm and what do you think has been your ... or would be your greatest ambition?
First passer-by:	My greatest ambition would be to go to Indonesia and see the wonderful arts and dances and musics of that country.
Interviewer:	Oh yes, fascinating. Er ...what's been your greatest achievement so far?
First passer-by:	My greatest achievement, well far be it from me to say but ... um ... I think that ... er ... I go back to the time that I got to Oxford. I was very very proud of ... of ... of finding myself at such a wonderful, hallowed ... er ... university of learning.
Interviewer:	Yes, I'm sure you were. What person do you admire most?
First passer-by:	Um ... Winston Churchill.
Interviewer:	Mmm, and who do you get on with best of all?
First passer-by:	My wife.
Interviewer:	Oh ...what was the nicest thing that happened to you yesterday?
First passer-by:	Yesterday ... gosh, I must say my memory ... isn't it awful ... er ... oh yes, my little girl came up to me first thing in the morning and she said, "Daddy, you're the most wonderful person in the world."
Interviewer:	Ha ha. Thank you very much.
First passer-by:	Thank you.
Interviewer:	Excuse me, could I ask you a few questions?
Second Passer-by:	Oh ... yes, all right.
Interviewer:	The first one is: What do you enjoy most in life?
Second passer-by:	Um ... well, I ... I'm sorry to be boring but ... er ... I really enjoy sitting in front of a fire and just reading by myself.
Interviewer:	That's lovely, isn't it? Yes, and what's your greatest ambition?
Second passer-by:	Um ... er ... to have as much money as possible. I don't mean to be enormously rich but to be ... have enough not to have to worry.
Interviewer:	Oh yes, and what do you think has been your greatest achievement?
Second passer-by:	Oh, having my daughter. I've got one little girl and it's her.
Interviewer:	Oh, lovely. Which person do you admire most?
Second passer-by:	Oh ... er ... um ... well either something quite frivolous like ... like an actor, like Laurence Olivier or ... No, really somebody like ... er ... Mahatma Gandhi, I think.

Interviewer:	Oh yes. And who do you get on with best of all?
Second passer-by:	Oh, my daughter—she's awfully nice to me, ha ha.
Interviewer:	Ha ha, lovely. What was the nicest thing that happened to you yesterday?
Second passer-by:	Well ... um ... we went out for a very nice walk and ... and saw a castle and it was just lovely, the whole day.
Interviewer:	Oh, it sounds super! Thank you very much.
Second passer-by:	Thank you.
Interviewer:	Excuse me ... er ... can I interrupt you for a moment?
Third passer-by:	Oh, yeah.
Interviewer:	Would you mind answering a few questions? The f ... the first one is: What do you enjoy most in life?
Third passer-by:	Oh well, I think I enjoy my work most.
Interviewer:	Mmm ... and what's your greatest ambition?
Third passer-by:	Greatest ambition. I think that would be to go on a safari in East Africa.
Interviewer:	Oh, that sounds wonderful. What's been your greatest achievement?
Third passer-by:	Well, I guess raising three daughters.
Interviewer:	Uhuh. Which person do you admire most?
Third passer-by:	Mmm ... I'd better say my wife! Ha ha.
Interviewer:	And who do you get on with best of all?
Third passer-by:	Well, I ... I'm sure: my wife.
Interviewer:	Again, your wife. And what was the nicest thing that happened to you yesterday?
Third passer-by:	Yesterday. Oh yes, yesterday was Sunday and we went for ... um ... a drive out in the country and I think that was just wonderful.
Interviewer:	Thank you very much. Thank you, goodbye.
Third passer-by:	Bye.

Task c

Interviewer:	Good morning, sir. I'm from radio station QRX, and I wonder if you'd mind answering a few questions for our survey today.
David:	Uh ... sure, why not?
Interviewer:	What's your name?
David:	Uh, my name is David George.

Interviewer:	David, what do you do for a living?
David:	I'm a professional baseball player.
Interviewer:	Really?
David:	Mm-hmm.
Interviewer:	That's terrific. What do you do for fun?
David:	Well, I like to read the classics—you know, Dickens, Shakespeare, ... uh ... books like that.
Interviewer:	Fabulous. And what's the most exciting thing that's happened to you recently?
David:	Just call me Dad. My wife and I ... uh ... had our first baby.
Interviewer:	Oh, (Yeah. A little girl.) that's wonderful.
David:	Mm-hmm.
Interviewer:	Who do you admire most in this world?
David:	Well, I admire my wife ... uh ... She's terrific. She's going to be a great mother, great mother.
Interviewer:	Terrific. What do you want to be doing five years from now?
David:	Well, ... uh ... five years from now I'd like to be a father of five. I'd like to have lots of kids around the house.
Interviewer:	That's fabulous.
David:	Yeah.
Interviewer:	Thanks very much for talking to us, David.
David:	Well, thank you.
Interviewer:	Good morning. I'm from radio station QRX, and I wondered if you'd mind answering a few questions today for our survey.
Suzanne:	Not at all.
Interviewer:	What's your name?
Suzanne:	Suzanne Brown.
Interviewer:	Suzanne, what do you do for a living?
Suzanne:	I'm a lawyer.
Interviewer:	A lawyer? And what do you do for fun?
Suzanne:	I like to run.
Interviewer:	Uh-huh. Running, like— ...
Suzanne:	Jogging.
Interviewer:	Jogging. And what's the most exciting thing that's happened to you recently?
Suzanne:	I got to run in the Boston Marathon.

Recording Script

Interviewer:	Congratulations. And who do you admire most in the world?
Suzanne:	Oh, well, I'd have to say Martin Luther King, Jr.
Interviewer:	Mmm, yes. And what do you want to be doing five years from today?
Suzanne:	Well, dare I say win the Boston Marathon?
Interviewer:	Wonderful. Thanks a lot for talking to us today, Suzanne.
Suzanne:	You're welcome.
Interviewer:	Good morning, sir. I'm from radio station QRX, and I wonder if you could answer a few questions for our survey this morning.
Adolfo:	Oh, yes, yes.
Interviewer:	What's your name?
Adolfo:	My name is Adolfo Vasquez.
Interviewer:	Adolfo, what do you do for a living?
Adolfo:	I'm a dancer.
Interviewer:	A dancer. And what do you do for fun?
Adolfo:	I watch ... uh ... musical movies.
Interviewer:	Musical movies. And what's the most exciting thing that's happened to you recently?
Adolfo:	Oh, about six years ago I moved to United States, (Uh-huh.) and that's quite exciting for me.
Interviewer:	Yes, that's very exciting. What do you—who do you admire most in the world?
Adolfo:	I admire a lot ... um ... Sophia Loren, the movie actress.
Interviewer:	I understand completely. (Mm-hmm.) What do you want to be doing five years from now?
Adolfo:	I like very much what I'm doing right now, so I really would like to keep doing it.
Interviewer:	Very good. (Mm-hmm.) Thanks for speaking to us today, Adolfo.
Adolfo:	Okay. You're welcome.
Interviewer:	Good morning, miss. I'm from radio station QRX, and I wonder if you could answer a few questions for our survey.
Linda:	Sure.
Interviewer:	What's your name?
Linda:	Linda Montgomery.
Interviewer:	Linda, what do you do for a living?
Linda:	Uh, well, right now I'm going to beauty school.

Interviewer:	Beauty school?
Linda:	Yeah.
Interviewer:	Uh-huh. And what do you do for fun?
Linda:	Oh, why for fun, I hang out with my friends—you know, go for pizza, stuff like that.
Interviewer:	I understand. What's the most exciting thing that's happened to you recently?
Linda:	Oh, this was so great! (Yeah?) Four of my friends and I, we went to a Bruce Springsteen concert. We actually—we got tickets.
Interviewer:	Wonderful.
Linda:	It was the best.
Interviewer:	Who do you admire most in the world?
Linda:	Who do I admi—I guess (Mm-hmm.) my dad, (Uh-huh.) probably my dad. Yeah.
Interviewer:	And what do you want to be doing five years from now?
Linda:	I would love it if I could have my own beauty salon.
Interviewer:	Uh-huh.
Linda:	That would be great.
Interviewer:	Thanks very much for talking to us today.
Linda:	OK.

Listening Two

Task b

Martin, Robert and Jean are being interviewed on the subject of friendship.

Interviewer:	How important are friends to you, Martin?
Martin:	I've never had a lot of friends. I've never regarded them as particularly important. Perhaps that's because I come from a big family. Two brothers and three sisters. And lots of cousins. And that's what's really important to me. My family. The different members of my family. If you really need help, you get it from your family, don't you? Well, at least that's what I've always found.
Interviewer:	What about you, Jean?
Jean:	To me friendship ... having friends, people I know I can really count on ... to me that's the most important thing in life. It's more important

Recording Script

	even than love. If you love someone, you can always fall out of love again, and that can lead to a lot of hurt feelings, bitterness, and so on. But a good friend is a friend for life.
Interviewer:	And what exactly do you mean by a friend?
Jean:	Well, I've already said, someone you know you can count on. I suppose what I really mean is ... let's see, how am I going to put this ... it's someone who will help you if you need help, who'll listen to you when you talk about your problems ... someone you can trust.
Interviewer:	What do you mean by a friend, Robert?
Robert:	Someone who likes the same things that you do, who you can argue with and not lose your temper, even if you don't always agree about things. I mean someone who you don't have to talk to all the time but can be silent with, perhaps. That's important, too. You can just sit together and not say very much sometimes. Just relax. I don't like people who talk all the time.
Interviewer:	Are you very good at keeping in touch with your friends if you don't see them regularly?
Robert:	No, not always. I've lived in lots of places, and, to be honest, once I move away, I often do drift out of touch with my friends. And I'm not a very good letter writer, either. Never have been. But I know that if I saw those friends again, if I ever moved back to the same place, or for some other reason we got back into close contact again, I'm sure the friendship would be just as strong as it was before.
Jean:	Several of my friends have moved away, got married, things like that. One of my friends has had a baby recently, and I'll admit I don't see her or hear from her as much as I used to ... She lives in another neighbourhood and when I phone her, she always seems busy. But that's an exception. I write a lot of letters to my friends and get a lot of letters from them. I have a friend I went to school with and ten years ago she emigrated to Canada, but she still writes to me every month, and I write to her just as often.

Task c

Girl:	So, how long have you been here?
Boy:	I've been here er just a couple of days actually; I haven't been here long at all. I'm on a big er big journey, round, you know I'm going all over the place.

What about you?

Girl: Well, I ... I live in Portugal, but I've (yeh?) been here now two weeks and I'm staying for a month.

Boy: Oh, wonderful, you see ... coming down here's like for you a summer holiday?

Girl: Yes, I come every year I come for a month, and you know, we have a nice time here.

Boy: Oh ... where do you live ... up in Lisbon or somewhere like that?

Girl: Yes ... (laugh) yes, I do.

Boy: (Laugh) ... how did I guess? Well, I'm just, I'm just on this big journey, you know ... around about. I'm just freewheeling for a bit.

Girl: Where're you from?

Boy: Australia, from Sydney (Goodness!) ... yes ... yeah, I was at university, you know, I just finished and er, though I'd go off round the world for a bit.

Girl: What a long way to go ... that's ... you have a long holiday, then, because, you know, to ... you ... ?

Boy: Well, I've finished studies you know ... I ... I haven't started work yet, so I thought I'd just take some time—however long it takes—to go round the world (Oh marvellous!) If I need some money, I just work where I am, you know (Ah, ah) But at the moment, I'm just here having a holiday up the campsite—wonderful here. I've, I've just arrived in Europe—a couple of weeks ago. I went to France and er ... I came round er through the United States, and I went right across the States and er I've come across to Europe now, France, now Portugal.

Girl: Oh, wonderful!

Boy: Yes, I'm just going really places where the windsurfing's good, cos that's er, that's what I like to do best.

Girl: You windsurf?

Boy: Yeah, yeah.

Girl: Goodness, so do I. We've got our boards and things over there.

Boy: Hey fantastic! Oh well, let's all go out together.

Girl: You should ... we should sometime. Oh, goodness, that's a coincidence?

Boy: Wonderful!

Girl: You must tell us all about your travels'cos we're all very interested yeah.

Boy: Well, there's not much to tell really.

Girl: But erm, listen maybe if you like, you can come over and have supper with us and er ...

Boy: Oh that would be lovely.

Girl: Well, you can tell us all about your stories and you ... we can make you a very nice meal, how about that?

Boy: ... would be marvellous ... a wonderful Portuguese meal ... a real Portuguese meal, how lovely, that'd be marvellous ...

Girl: Good.

Unit 3 City and Country

Listening One

Task b

Chairman: We're here tonight in the lovely Suffolk village of Tuddenham, where we're the guests of the Tuddenham Women's Institute. Our team tonight is Henry Mitchell, the Canadian broadcaster and writer, Mary Johnson, the actress, and Jenny Martin, the journalist. And our first question comes from ...

Villager: Janet Parker. If the members of the team could choose where to live, would they live in a village or in a city?

Chairman: Thank you, Mrs. Parker.

Villager: Miss!

Chairman: Sorry ... er ... Miss Parker. If the members of the team could choose where to live, would they live in a village or in a city? Henry.

Henry: Well, I think I'd prefer to live in a village because ... well, I think the people are friendly and there's a lot of fresh air. I think life generally is healthier in a village and I like being close to nature. And it's very easy for my work as a writer to have peace and quiet.

Chairman: Mary.

Mary: Well, I'd prefer to live in a city because there's more going on. Er ... being an actress, I need to go to the cinema and the theatre and there's far more entertainment in the city than there is in the country, of course. I also like it because ... um ... people are more open-minded. People don't ... um ... mind what you do in the city. And for the shopping as well, I mean, I love going to the village shop but the stores and shops in

	London can't compare with anything.
Chairman:	You don't think the ... er ... the city can be lonely?
Mary:	Oh, no, no. You can ... have to go out and make friends. And ...
Chairman:	Good, fine.
Mary:	... at least there's the opportunity in London.
Chairman:	Jenny.
Jenny:	Yes, well, I prefer living in a village. It's safer than a city and there's less crime and of course there's less traffic, so it's much more pleasant. Then, it's much cheaper than the city. You know, rents are cheaper and so of course are house prices. It's quiet, it's ... it's peaceful. Yes, I much prefer living in a village.
Chairman:	Jolly good, all right. Well, thank you very much indeed. And let's find out where the members of the team really do live. Henry?
Henry:	Well, I live in London because I have to do a lot of travelling and it's more convenient, but I don't like living there.
Chairman:	Fine. Er ... Mary?
Mary:	Oh, I live in a village rather like this one—because my husband is a farmer.
Chairman:	I see, but you'd ... er ... you don't really like that situation?
Mary:	I'm afraid I don't!
Chairman:	Oh dear, oh dear, Jenny?
Jenny:	Yes, well I have the best of both worlds, I'm afraid. I live in a small town which is within easy reach of London and it's very close to the country.
Chairman:	Mmm, very nice too. OK, well, thank you very much. And our next question is from ...

Task d

Jean:	So how do you like our city?
Janice:	Oh, I love it—it's so exciting. Don't you agree, Ben?
Ben:	... Yes, it is exciting ... but it's too noisy and dirty for me.
Jean:	Well, what do you think of the sights?
Ben:	Oh, they're amazing—especially the skyscrapers.
Janice:	I prefer the monuments. I think the Statue of Liberty is beautiful.
Jean:	Yes, it is. OK, now what's your opinion of transport in the city?
Ben:	At the moment we're using taxis. They're not too bad.
Janice:	Well, they're very expensive.

Jean:	What about the subway?
Janice:	Oh, I hate it. We had a ride on it yesterday—it was terribly dirty.
Ben:	Oh, I think it's all right. Anyway, it's very cheap.
Jean:	Right. OK, can you tell me where you're staying?
Janice:	Uh, hang on, the address is in my bag ... here ... 103 East 49th Street. The Hotel Metropolitan.
Jean:	Do you like it?
Ben:	Oh no, I think it's awful—I prefer older hotels.
Janice:	Well, I like it!
Jean:	Fine, now can you write your names on the questionnaire, please? Here's a pen.
Ben:	OK.
Jean:	Thanks, that's great. And when are you returning to England?
Janice:	We're flying back on Saturday.
Jean:	Well, enjoy the rest of your stay!
Ben:	Thanks.
Jean:	Bye bye.

Listening Two
Task b

Customer:	Hi. Um ... I'd like to take a trip to Frankfurt for a couple of days. Can you tell me the best way to get there from Paris?
Travel Agent:	Well, of course the fastest way is to fly. (Uh-huh.) It takes about an hour. And there are ten or eleven flights a day.
Customer:	Oh, well, that sounds quick and convenient.
Travel Agent:	But you have to remember that you have to go from Paris to the airport, and when once you arrive in Frankfurt you have to go from the airport to the city. And that will add about three hours to your trip.
Customer:	Oh, I hadn't thought of that. Still, four hours traveling time isn't bad. Uh ... How much does it cost?
Travel Agent:	Wait. Let me check. It is nine hundred and three francs one way, (Mm-hmm.) which is about a hundred and thirty dollars, and eighteen hundred and seven francs round trip, which comes to about two hundred and sixty dollars.
Customer:	Two hundred and sixty dollars? Sounds kind of expensive for only

	two days in Frankfurt. Uh, what about the train? I mean, it must be cheaper, but how long does that take?
Travel Agent:	It takes ... uh ... six hours. But that is (Uh-huh.) much cheaper. (Yeah.) Uh ... second class is three hundred and thirty-eight francs one way, about (Hm-hmm.) fifty dollars, and six hundred and seventy-six francs round trip, which comes to ninety-eight dollars. And you have three direct trains a day.
Customer:	I bet it's a beautiful trip this time of year.
Travel Agent:	Oh, I'm sure. And then it's as comfortable as an airplane. And (Uh-huh.) it arrives right in the center of Frankfurt.
Customer:	Great. Wha ... What about buses or other ways to get there?
Travel Agent:	Buses, ... uh ... now, I'm not sure. You would have to change several times, and it would take about thirteen hours. No, but what you could do is rent a car. And I could get you a very good deal: two hundred and forty francs a day, about thirty-five dollars, with unlimited mileage. And then you'd have the advantage of having the car to get around in Frankfurt.
Customer:	Unlimited mileage? Well, how long do you think it would ... uh ... take to drive from Paris to Frankfurt?
Travel Agent:	If you take the highways, seven to eight hours.
Customer:	It would be fun, though, to pick my own route. And I bet it would be scenic, too. Then of course, it is a long drive, and I don't want to be tired when I arrive. ... Look, I'll have ... I'll have to think about it. And I'll ... I'll be sure to, you know, call you in a day or two. Thank you for your help.
Travel Agent:	Fine, fine. Goodbye.

Unit 4 Marriage

Listening One

Task b

(George Hayes goes to the Find Your Partner Agency)

Smother:	Good morning! Good morning! Come in, come in.

Recording Script

Hayes:	Er, thank you ... good morning.
Smother:	Good morning, sit down, please, sit down. Now then, what is your name?
Hayes:	Hayes, George Hayes.
Smother:	Well-George-tell me about your ideal wife!
Hayes:	Oh ... er, what do I say?
Smother:	Well, do you like tall women, short women, old women, young women? We've got all of them you know!
Hayes:	Well I like short women. Yes, my ideal wife is short. I'm short, you know.
Smother:	Yes, I can see that.
Hayes:	And ... er ... my ideal wife has brown eyes ... and, well, a happy face.
Smother:	A happy face?
Hayes:	Yes.
Smother:	Yes. Well now ... short woman, brown eyes ... happy face.
Smother:	Hello! Hello! Come in. Sit down!
Orchard:	Thank you.
Smother:	And you are?
Orchard:	Fenella Orchard. I want a husband.
Smother:	I see. Tell me about your ideal husband.
Orchard:	Well, my ideal husband is tall and thin ...
Smother:	Tall and thin ...
Orchard:	With blonde ... no, grey hair and blue eyes.
Smother:	Yes, well they all want one of those.
Smother:	And what's your name?
Richards:	Stella. Stella Richards.
Smother:	Hello, Stella.
Richards:	Hello.
Smother:	Well, here at Find Your Partner we're ready to help you find your ideal husband. What does he look like, Stella?
Richards:	Mmm ... well ... can he have a beard?
Smother:	A beard?
Richards:	And glasses.
Smother:	And glasses.
Richards:	And he'd better be short.

Smother:	Okay. So your ideal husband would be a short man with a beard and glasses?
Richards:	Yes.
Smother:	Good morning! Welcome to Find Your Partner. Er ... come in ... sit down.
Winterton:	Thank you young man.
Smother:	Please ... please sit down, Mr. ... er ...
Winterton:	Winterton. Albert Winterton.
Smother:	Yes, Mr. Winterton?
Winterton:	I'm looking for a new wife.
Smother:	Ah, you're looking for a new wife.
Winterton:	Yes. I want a tall, thin one with blue eyes and blond hair.
Smother:	Er ... yes ... a tall thin woman with blue eyes and blond hair. Excuse me, Mr. Winterton, But ... er ... how old are you?
Winterton:	A hundred and four.

Task c

Announcer:	All right, Sonia. You know the rules to our game.
Sonia:	Mm-hmm.
Announcer:	You have a few minutes to ask the bachelors anything you want. And then when the time is up you'll have to make your choice, okay?
Sonia:	Okay.
Announcer:	Okay, let's begin.
Sonia:	Bachelor number one, what do you do for a living?
Bachelor No. 1:	Well, I'm ... uh ... vice-president of Ace Construction Company. In fact, you know, I'm the youngest vice-president in the company's history.
Sonia:	Mm-hmm. Bachelor number two, what do you do for a living?
Bachelor No. 2:	Well. Sonia, ... uh ... I'm a composer. Uh ... I make my living writing music for commercials and films, and ... and sometimes television shows.
Sonia:	Thank you. Bachelor number three, what do you do for a living?
Bachelor No. 3:	Well, Sonia, I'm an airline pilot for ... uh ...International American Airlines now for five years.
Sonia:	Bachelor number one, what do you like to do in your free time?

Recording Script

Bachelor No. 1:	Well, Sonia, in my free time I like to … uh … gamble, drive my sports car—it is a Ferrari—and … uh … date beautiful women like you, Sonia.
Sonia:	Uh-huh. Bachelor number two, what do you like to do in your free time?
Bachelor No. 2:	Oh, well … uh … I like to have a wonderful woman come over to my apartment and cook a real nice dinner, … uh … open a great bottle of wine, and then I like to play the piano and sing some of my songs for her.
Sonia:	Thank you. Bachelor number three, what do you like to do in your free time?
Bachelor No. 3:	Well, Sonia, I like out … outdoor activities. I … like to ski, hike, play tennis, bike.
Sonia:	Thank you. Bachelor number one, what do you think is your best quality?
Bachelor No. 1:	Well, it's hard to narrow it down to just one. I mean, I'm good-looking; I'm intelligent, ambitious, witty, rich certainly, and …
Sonia:	Uh-huh. Bachelor number two, what do you think is your best quality?
Bachelor No. 2:	Uh. Mmm. Best quality? It's … it's … hard to say. Uh … well … uh … I'm a good listener, and … uh … and I'm … I'm interested in other people.
Sonia:	Mm-hmm. Thanks. Bachelor number three, what is your best quality?
Bachelor No. 3:	I'd have to say I'm dependable. I'm reliable. I'll always be there if you need me, Sonia.
Sonia:	Okay. Bachelor number two, what is your least attractive characteristic? I'm not going to ask number one, because I'm sure he doesn't have any.
Bachelor No. 2:	Uh … well … uh … well I like to stay up all night and sleep during the day. So … uh … my schedule isn't always easy to live with.
Sonia:	Mm-hmm. Bachelor number three, what is your least attractive characteristic?
Bachelor No. 3:	Honestly, I'd have to say, I have a quick temper.
Sonia:	Uh-huh.
Bachelor No. 3:	I don't keep things in.
Announcer:	Sonia, gentlemen, I'm afraid I'm going to have to break in here.

That's all the time we have. Now it's time for you to decide. Will it be Bachelor number one, Bachelor number two, or Bachelor number three?

Listening Two

Task a

Mr. Markman is writing an article for a women's magazine about marriage. Listen to this interview he recorded with Mrs. Gold.

Mr. Markham (Interviewer):	Mrs. Gold. You know a lot about marriage, don't you?
Mrs. Gold:	Yes, I certainly do. That's right.
Mr. Markham (Interviewer):	How many times have you been married in fact?
Mrs. Gold:	Three times. I've been married three times. Yes, that's right.
Mr. Markham (Interviewer):	How old were you when you first got married?
Mrs. Gold:	Oh, I was ever so young. I was only seventeen. Too young really.
Mr. Markham (Interviewer):	You think you were too young?
Mrs. Gold:	Yes, I do. Definitely. I only got married 'cause I didn't want to live at home with my Mum and Dad.
Mr. Markham (Interviewer):	What was your first marriage like?
Mrs. Gold:	We were both too young really. And we didn't have any money. George, that was his name, worked hard though. He tried to make a good life for us, but we went out a lot. He loved going out and meeting people and so we spent everything we earned. And then I had Mary, my first child. So there was never enough money. He was a lovely man though, considerate and fun to be with. We had a lot of laughs together.
Mr. Markham (Interviewer):	What happened to him?
Mrs. Gold:	Oh, it was terrible. Do you remember the Docanster train crash? That was him ... he was the driver. They took him to hospital, but he never regained consciousness.
Mr. Markham (Interviewer):	That's terrible. I'm sorry.
Mrs. Gold:	Oh, it all happened a long time ago and then Fred

Recording Script

	came along. Fred was ever so good-looking. I thought I was lucky when he asked me to marry him. But he was so different from George. He lost his job after we'd been married six months and then never tried to get another one. He never helped in the house and was terribly untidy. He just wanted a wife to give him meals, wash his clothes and keep the house clean. Then he started drinking and came home drunk. Sometimes he didn't even come home, as well. Then the next day he'd come home with lipsticks on his shirt collar and ask me to wash it.
Mr. Markham (Interviewer):	How did the marriage finish?
Mrs. Gold:	Well, I just had to leave him in the end. He became so violent when he got home drunk that I went and lived with my mother for a while—till the divorce.
Mr. Markham (Interviewer):	How old were you when you got the divorce?
Mrs. Gold:	Well, I was still young, I think I was about 32. I was still an attractive woman then.
Mr. Markham (Interviewer):	And your third husband?
Mrs. Gold:	Arthur? I suppose you could say that he's the ideal husband. He's got a good job, helps in the house, doesn't drink much and is very good with the children. We get on very well with each other.
Mr. Markham (Interviewer):	So. What do you think are the most important qualities a husband should have?
Mrs. Gold:	He should be like a very good friend. Someone you can talk to and who understands you and tries to help. He should work hard but most important know how to enjoy life.

Task c

Interviewer:	Do you mind if I ask you why you've never got married?
Dennis:	Uh ... well, that isn't easy to answer.
Interviewer:	Is it that you've never met the right woman? Is that it?
Dennis:	I don't know. Several times I have met a woman who seemed "right", as you say. But for some reason it's never worked out.

Interviewer:	No? Why not?
Dennis:	Hmm. I'm not really sure.
Interviewer:	Well, could you perhaps describe what happened with one of these women?
Dennis:	Uh ... yes, there was Cynthia, for example.
Interviewer:	And what kind of woman was she?
Dennis:	Intelligent. Beautiful. She came from the right social background, as well. I felt I really loved her. But then something happened.
Interviewer:	What?
Dennis:	I found out that she was still seeing an old boyfriend of hers.
Interviewer:	Was that so bad? I mean, why did you ... why did you feel that...
Dennis:	She had told me that her relationship was all over, which ... uh ... which was a lie.
Interviewer:	Are you saying that it was because she had lied to you that you decided to break off the relationship?
Dennis:	Yes, yes, exactly ... Obviously, when I found out that she had lied to me, I simply couldn't ... uh ... well, I simply couldn't trust her any more. And of course that meant that we couldn't possibly get married.
Interviewer:	Uh huh. I see. At least, I think I do. But...you said there were several women who seemed "right".
Dennis:	Yes.
Interviewer:	Well ... what happened the other times?
Dennis:	Well, once I met someone who I think I loved very deeply but ... unfortunately, she didn't share my religious views.
Interviewer:	Your religious views?
Dennis:	Yes, I expect the woman I finally marry to agree with me on such ... such basic things as that.
Interviewer:	I see.
Dennis:	Does that sound old-fashioned?
Interviewer:	Uh ... no. Not necessarily. What was her name, by the way?
Dennis:	Sarah.
Interviewer:	Do you think you'll ever meet someone who meets ... uh ... how shall I say it ... who meets all your ... requirements?
Dennis:	I don't know. How can I? But I do feel it's important not to ... not to just drift into ... a relationship, simply because I might be lonely.
Interviewer:	Are you lonely?

Recording Script

Dennis: Sometimes. Aren't we all? But I know that I can live alone, if necessary. And I think I would far prefer to do that ... to live alone ... rather than to marry somebody who isn't really ... uh ... well, really what I'm looking for ... what I really want.

Task d

Professor: OK, class, now, this week we will be looking at family life around the world. Therefore, today I would like to begin by focusing on marriage.

All societies have their own form of marriage. The ideas that we have about marriage are part of the cultural background. Now, one of the obvious challenges for most people is to find the right person to marry.

As we study marriage, we find that different cultures have solved the problem of finding a marriage partner, or spouse, in different ways. Finding a marriage partner has never been easy for people, no matter when or where they have lived.

In China in the first half of the 1900s, marriage decisions were often made by parents or older family members. This practice is known as arranged marriage. Parents who wanted to find a spouse for their son or daughter asked a matchmaker to find someone with the right characteristics, including age and educational background. According to the Chinese way of thinking at that time, it might be a serious mistake to let two young people choose their own partners. This important decision was made by older family members, who understood that the goal of marriage was to produce healthy sons. Sons were considered to be important because they would take positions of leadership in the family and keep the family name alive.

Today, however, couples in China meet, they fall in love, and then they get married—as couples do in most other cultures around the world. But arranged marriages are not completely a thing of the past. You see, sometimes, in modern-day India, marriage partners are still matched by their families. And some couples only meet each other two or three times before the wedding day.

In contrast, in some traditions, young people were more involved in choosing a partner. For example, the Hopi, a native people of North America, had a very different idea about finding a marriage partner. The Hopi allowed boys to leave their parents' home at age thirteen to live in a kiva, a special home for young males. Here they enjoyed the freedom to go out along at night and secretly visit young girls. Boys typically left the girl's home before daylight, but a girl's parents usually did not get angry about the night visits. They allowed the visits to continue if they thought the boy would make a good marriage partner. After a few months of visits, most girls became pregnant. In this way, the girls were choosing their favorite boy for a husband.

Now, let me just stop here for a moment and ask if you have any questions before I continue ...

Unit 5   Keep in Touch

Listening One

Task b

Secretary:	Mr. Turner's office.
Caller #1:	Hello. I'd like to speak to Mr. Turner, please.
Secretary:	I'm sorry, he's in a meeting right now. May I take a message?
Caller #1:	Uh, yes. This is Mary Roberts from the First National Bank. Would you ask him to call me at 772-1852?
Secretary:	Okay. That's 772-18-?
Caller #1:	52.
Secretary:	Okay.
Caller #1:	He can reach me at this number until, say, twelve thirty, or between two and five this afternoon.
Secretary:	That's fine, Ms. Roberts. I'll tell him. I'll give him your message.
Caller #1:	Thank you very much. Goodbye.
Secretary:	Goodbye. ... Mr. Turner's office.
Caller #2:	Yes. Hello. Is Mr. Turner in, please?
Secretary:	No, I'm sorry, he's at a meeting right now. May I take a message?
Caller #2:	This is Mr. Brown calling. I have a lunch appointment with Mr. Turner for tomorrow noon that I have to cancel. I'm going to be out of town for a while. Would you offer my apologies to Mr. Turner and have him call me, please, to reschedule? My number here is 743-9821.
Secretary:	Okay, Mr. Brown. I'll make sure he gets the message.
Caller #2:	Thank you so much.
Secretary:	You're welcome.
Caller #2:	Bye-bye, now.
Secretary:	Bye-bye. ... Mr. Turner's office.
Caller #3:	Hello, Jane. Is my husband in?

Recording Script

Secretary:	Oh, no, Mrs. Turner. I'm sorry. He's in a meeting until noon.
Caller #3:	Oh.
Secretary:	Oh, excuse me just a minute. I have another call. Can you hold for a second?
Caller #3:	Yes, sure.
Secretary:	Mr. Turner's office. Will you hold please? Hello, Mrs. Turner. Uh ... Would you like your husband to call you back?
Caller #3:	No, that's not necessary. But would you just tell him, please, that I won't be home until eight o'clock? I'll be working late.
Secretary:	Oh, sure. I'll tell him.
Caller #3:	Thanks a lot. Bye-bye.
Secretary:	Bye-bye. Thank you for holding. Uh... Can I help you?
Caller #4:	Yeah. Hi. This is Wendy at Travel Agents International. Umm ... I've got Mr. Turner booked on a flight for Puerto Rico next Tuesday. Can you take down the information?
Secretary:	Sure.
Caller #4:	Okay. It's Pan Am Flight two twenty-six, which leaves Tuesday the twelfth at eight a.m.
Secretary:	Okay. That's Pan Am Flight two twenty-six, leaving Tuesday the twelfth at eight a.m.
Caller #4:	Right. Umm ... I'll send the ticket over later this afternoon, if that's okay.
Secretary:	Oh, sure. That'd be fine.
Caller #4:	Okay. Thanks a lot. Bye.
Secretary:	Bye-bye. ... Mr. Turner's office.
Caller #5:	Hello. Uh ... My name is Juan Salvador. I'm calling from Puerto Rico, and I want to speak to Mr. Turner.
Secretary:	I'm sorry, sir, Mr. Turner is in a meeting. May I take a message?
Caller #5:	I ... think it would be better if I ... uh ... call him later. Uh ... Will you please tell me when he's going to be free?
Secretary:	He'll be free in about an hour.
Caller #5:	Oh, thanks. Uh ... Why don't you leave him a message saying that I called him and I will called him back? It's in regard to our meeting on next Wednesday.
Secretary:	Okay. Uh ... Could you give me your name again, please?
Caller #5:	Yes, of course. Juan Salvador.
Secretary:	Could you spell that, please?

Caller #5: Yes. S-a-l-v-a-

Secretary: Uh ... Excuse me, sir. I'm having trouble hearing you. Could you repeat it, please?

Caller #5: Yes, of course. S-a-l-v-a-d-o-r.

Secretary: Thank you very much, Mr. Salvador. I'll give Mr. Turner the message.

Caller #5: Oh, thank you very much. Bye-bye.

Secretary: Bye-bye.

Task c

Caller #1: Hello. My name is Jeff Jones. And I'm calling about my Horizon. Is it ready yet? ... It's red ... What, it's not—it's not ready yet? ... Well excuse me, but you people promised me that this would be ready today. ... What ...? It needs a new engine? Oh, come on, I can't believe that ... It'll cost how much? ... No, no. Please, please. There ... there's got to be some mistake. Could you please check once more? ... No, it's a red Horizon, not orange. Nineteen eighty-two model ... Oh, thank God. I guess you did have the wrong one. Okay. Well, when can I pick it up? ... You have-what? You haven't started working on it? ... No, wait now—excuse ... no, wait a minute. You promised me that this would be ready today, and I need it for a trip first thing in the morning ... All right. Thank you. All right. Thank you. Now, ... uh ... I'll be there at four thirty to pick it up. Is that fine? ... All right. Goodbye.

Caller #2: Hello? ... No, Mark isn't home. Uh ... would you like to leave a message? ... Hold on just a second. Let me get a pencil ... Okay. Go ahead ... Mary says she'll be expecting you at nine o'clock. Um ... wait a minute. Uh ... who are you? I mean, what is this about? What are you meeting him at nine o'clock for? ... Yes, it does concern me ... No, I'm not his sister, I'm his wife. How do you know Mark? ... You met where? ... Wait a minute. Do you mean Mark Smith, Mark Smith on Harley Street? ... Oh, you want Mark Smith on Harwood Street. Oh. Uh ... no, it's an easy mistake to make. Uh ... sure, sure-no, it's fine. Bye.

Caller #3: Hi. You busy? ... What did you think of that little scene we had this morning? Is that what you heard? Let me tell you what really happened, okay? I mean, everybody knows I'm there half an hour early every morning, right? But today I got struck on the bus. I got there five minutes late. Big deal. She actually had the nerve to tell me to watch it and be

Recording Script

	on time tomorrow. Can you believe it? She drives me crazy ... You too? ... She actually said that to you? ... Who does she think she is? She's only been there a couple of months longer than we have. She ... she acts like she's running the whole show ... She asked you to type a letter for her today? I can't believe it. I hope you said no. She doesn't have the authority to ask you to do work for her. The next time you just tell her to go to ... yeah, I think she's stuck up. I just hope that something happens real soon, because I can't stand it much longer ... Oh. Okay. I'll let you go. Lunch tomorrow? ... Great. Bye.
Caller #4:	Hi. It's me ... Li ... li ... listen. I'm sorry about last night ... You ... you know, I've really been looking forward to seeing you. Uh ... you know, with the long hours I've been working, it's been hard for us to get together ... I ... I know. I'm sorry. I didn't mean to lose my temper. No, I didn't say that. That's not what I ... I meant. Well, naturally I was jealous when I saw you with that ... wha ... I did not. Yeah, but how was I supposed to know that? ... Uh ... listen, listen. I ... uh ... I just called to apologise and say I'm sorry. You know, ... uh ... it would hurt if you said ... uh ... you're sorry to me, too, you know ... Okay. Goodbye.

Listening Two

Task a

Morning, Julie. I won't be in today; er ... hopefully I'll see you in the morning. Would you mind writing to Jennifer O'Brien and tell her she's got the job? "Dear Miss O'Brien, we are pleased to make you an offer of employment at MEDCO Clinic, Jeddah, stop. A copy of the contract is enclosed, stop. May we have your acceptance in writing as soon as possible? Stop. Paragraph. This offer is subject to a satisfactory medical examination, stop. Would you please telephone our office to arrange an appointment with our medical officer? Stop. You will also need to bring your passport, ten passport-sized photographs, and the originals of your nursing certificates. Stop. Paragraph. We look forward to hearing from you, stop. Yours sincerely, Molley Keaveney." Oh, and we'd better write to Joan Ryan thanking her for attending the interview, but we regret to inform her on, on this occasion her application has been unsuccessful, blah, blah, blah. Oh, and phone those twits at the *Nursing Weekly* about the ad. for Kuwait. Er, the telephone number should read four six double six, not four six two six. Tell them to replace the ad. free of charge for one week.

And, erm, while you're on the phone, would you mind, er, placing an ad. for *Dental Nurse*, Riyadh, Saudi Arabia? One year contract, er, salary sixty thousand Saudi Riyals, that's six oh, tax free. Oh, and er, what else was there? Oh yes, could you give Jim a ring and ask him to fix the washbasin and have a look at the heater? And, erm, we need some more coffee; perhaps you could pop out at lunch time and get some. Er, and remember you get half an hour for lunch, madam. And don't forget to water the plants, please. See you tomorrow. Bye.

Task b

1.

Secretary:	Hello! Mr. Donaldson's secretary. Can I help you?
Caller:	Good morning. I'd like to make an appointment to see Mr. Donaldson on Friday, please.
Secretary:	Who's speaking please?
Caller:	James Smith.
Secretary:	Yes, Mr. Smith. Friday is all right. Would 12:15 be convenient?
Caller:	Thank you. That'll be fine.

2.

Secretary:	Hello. Professor Freeman's secretary. Can I help you?
Caller:	Good afternoon. I'd like to make an appointment to see the professor on Thursday, please.
Secretary:	Who's speaking please?
Caller:	Richard Jones.
Secretary:	Yes, Mr. Jones. Would 9:45 be convenient?
Caller:	Thank you. That'll be fine.

3.

Secretary:	Good morning. Dr. Nelson's secretary. Can I help you?
Caller:	Good morning. I'd like to make an appointment to see the doctor on Wednesday, please.
Secretary:	Who's speaking please?
Caller:	Ann Brown.
Secretary:	Thank you. Is 2:40 any good?
Caller:	That's fine. Thank you very much.

4.

Secretary:	Hello, can I help you?

Recording Script

Caller: I'd like to see Mrs. Harper on Tuesday, please.
Secretary: Who's speaking please?
Caller: David Sim.
Secretary: Yes, it'll have to be in the afternoon. Will 4:20 do?
Caller: That'll be fine. Many thanks.

Task c

1.

A: Well, I'm sorry, madam, there's nothing I can do. The manager's out just now ... He's the only one who can authorise it.
B: All right, just give me a credit note then.
A: I'm sorry, the only thing I can do is let you exchange it for something else of the same price. How about that? Otherwise, you'll have to come back next Monday and see the manager. I'm sure he'll be able to let you ...
B: Oh goodness, I don't know what to do. I'm only here on a visit and I'll be back home next week. ... Just a minute, what about if ... if you ...

2.

A: Well, well, well, if it isn't Mr. Thompson!
B: Ah ... ah ... I'm not sure that I ...
A: Oh come on, Mr. Thompson, surely you remember?
B: No, I'm afraid I ...
A: 1973? 4B?
B: Oh? Oh! 4B, let me see, ah yes. Young Watson, how are you, my boy?
A: No, no, it's Watkins, actually Bill Watkins.
B: William Watson. Ah, you were the who was expelled for ...
A: No, no, no I'm Watkins. Watson wasn't even in my form.
B: Watkins. Watkins. No, no, I'm sorry I don't know anyone ...

3.

A: Eat it up!
B: Shan't.
A: Eat it up this minute or you really will be in trouble.
B: Eat it up yourself.
A: Now look here, young lady, if you don't do what I say, I'll ...
B: If I do eat it up, I'll be sick. Then I'll probably die and then you'll be sorry.

A: All right, I'll eat it myself. Mmm, it's delicious!

B: No, it's mine! I want it!

4.

A: Same time next week, then.

B: Fine, and in the meanwhile I'll take care of things here.

A: Right. And if there's any trouble, let me know in the usual way.

B: Ok then. Goodbye. ... Oh, just a minute, I've been thinking.

A: What?

B: Look, I think we've got to change the signal. There's been a man hanging around outside my place and he could be on the other side.

A: All right. Make a yellow chalk mark at shoulder height on the north wall if you need to contact me earlier.

B: North wall, right. If everything's ok, I'll leave the usual mark on the south wall.

A: Good.

B: See you next week, then. And good luck!

5.

A: Finished yet?

B: No.

A: Going to take long?

B: Don't know.

A: Want any help?

B: No, not really. ... Listen, why don't you get on with your own?

A: Finished ages ago. Dead easy. Specially page 43.

B: 43, don't you mean 143?

A: No, 43. Why, have you been doing 143?

B: Yeah, I thought that's what she said.

A: No, course not!

B: Huh, I though it was a bit difficult.

6.

A: Ah ... is this seat free?

B: Yeah, there's no charge.

A: I mean can I sit here?

B: I expect so. It's a free country.

A: Thanks. It's a lovely day, isn't it?

B: No, not really, too dry.
A: Yes, I see what you mean. It is very dry. Um ... is the coffee any good here?
B: It's all right, yeah.
A: Er, Miss! Coffee, please ... Make that two coffees! Oh, are you ...?
B: Yeah, bye.
A: Oh, but I've just ordered ...

Unit 6   Habits

Listening One

Task b

A: Good morning, sir.
B: Good morning.
A: Would you mind if I asked you a few questions? We're doing a ...
B: Well I'm in a bit of a hurry.
A: Market survey. Well it won't take very long, really.
B: Well, all right.
A: ... be very grateful.
B: What's it all about?
A: Umm, well it's about your sleeping habits.
B: My sleeping habits?
A: Yes. Um ... Just a few questions.
B: It's a bit personal.
A: We ... we'll try and keep it—decent. Um—how much time every day do you spend um making the bed?
B: Well I don't make the bed. My wife makes the bed. She's always made the bed.
A: I see. Oh.
B: I don't think men should be making beds, do you?
A: Does she spend a long time doing it?
B: Oh we've got one of those er "duvet" things. I think you just throw it over.
A: I see.
B: Ha ... She makes a lot of fuss about making the bed but er ...
A: So not very long?

B: Not very long, no. I suppose about a minute or so.
A: Hm. What do you um do before you go to bed in the evening?
B: Well I, er, well, ha, that's a bit difficult isn't it?
A: Ha, ha.
B: I suppose er I read—sometimes.
A: Mm mm.
B: Sometimes I just flake out like that.
A: Mm. Thank you.
B: Er. Sometimes. Yeh, sometimes you know, talk and er, mess around, you know ...
A: Mm mm. And um, whe ... when you wake up in the morning do you ... What is the bed like?
B: What's the bed like?
A: Hm.
B: What do you mean, "what's the bed like?"
A: Um. Well I mean is it ...
B: Well. Looks as if somebody's been sleeping in it.
A: I see, yes.
B: All wrinkled, isn't it?
A: Very, very untidy?
B: Well not very untidy. I, I'm quite a quiet sleeper so they say.
A: Hm.
B: My wife isn't.
A: Hm. Your wife isn't?
B: No. Her side of the bed's always in much more of a mess than mine.
A: I see. Do you um, do you sleep well at night?
B: Oh yes. Straight out. No trouble at all.
A: But if, if you have a problem or if you can't sleep, what do you do?
B: If I have a problem? Well I um, try not to think about it I suppose.
A: I see, yes. You don't have a method for going to sleep?
B: Oh well, the old counting sheep and that?
A: Mm.
B: No, I just, er, try and think of something else, you know.
A: I see. And um, supposing ... do you, er, wake up sometimes in the middle of the night?
B: No, never. Well, unless somebody comes to the door or the telephone rings, no never.

A: Oh. I see. And, supposing you hear a strange noise in the night, what do you do?
B: Well ah. I'd go down and have a look round.
A: Very brave.
B: No. I'd, erm, I'd just be angry I think. Being disturbed. Worried about the house, you know.
A: Mm. Mm.
B: Wife to look after. Children ...
A: Mm. A responsible husband. And um, do you ...
B: Well I suppose you could say that, yes.
A: Do you have, er, complaints? Do people um, are people angry about the way you sleep?
B: I haven't had any complaints to date. No.
A: None at all?
B: No. I'd say I'm a very nice person to sleep with. Easy. Anything else?
A: Yes. The last question sir. Um. What sort of dreams do you have?
B: Well. Don't dream much actually.
A: Never?
B: Um. No. No. Can't say I dream. No, not very much.
A: What was the last dream you had?
B: Oh well. I always try and remember them when I wake up, if I've had a dream, and then it just goes ...
A: Mm.
B: I used to try writing them down or talking about them but my wife doesn't seem very interested now. Says my dreams aren't very interesting.
A: Oh dear. Oh.
B: So, er, well anyway.
A: Well maybe, maybe you could tell me about them? Anyway, then ... Thank you very much sir ...
B: Yeah maybe I might do that.
A: Thank you. Yes.
B: Right.
A: Goodbye.
B: Goodbye.

Task c

A: Good morning sir.

B: Er. Good morning.

A: I wonder if you'd like to answer a few questions?

B: Well er ...

A: We're doing a market survey.

B: That depends what sort of questions they are ah?

A: Well it's questions about your sleeping habits.

B: Sleeping habits?

A: Mm.

B: Well. I suppose that's all right. Yes. Well. What do you want to know?

A: Right. Um. What would you do if you heard a strange noise in the middle of the night?

B: I'd wonder what it was er I suppose and then I'd um see if it happened again.

A: Mm.

B: I would lay awake a little while, waiting to see if it happened again, and if it did—I suppose I'd get up ...

A: Mm.

B: And go and see what it was.

A: Very courageous. Um. If you, if you can't get to sleep at night, er, what do you, what do you do? Have you a special method?

B: Well I generally go to sleep straight away. I don't have any trouble getting to sleep.

A: Mm.

B: Well if I do have ... occasionally, happens about once every six months I suppose that I can't go to sleep and then I er ... I lie awake and I um think about things.

A: Mm. Mm. Think about things. And er what about before going to bed? What do you do before you go to bed?

B: Well I, depends, er if I've been out I, I, don't do anything, I just come home and go straight to bed. I clean my teeth. Ha. Ha.

A: Mm. Good. Good.

B: That's one thing I do before I go to bed. Um, well occasionally read a bit but if I read I go, I tend to go straight to sleep. I, I usually read about a page and then I go straight off.

Recording Script

A: Mm. Yes. Me too. Yeah. And um when you dream, what do you dream about?
B: Aah! Now that's a very interesting question.
A: Mm.
B: Yes. I've been dreaming a great deal recently as it happens.
A: Have you?
B: Mm.
A: Have you?
B: Um. I've had dreams every single ... all, all the way through my holidays. I've just come back from my holiday and I've been dreaming every single night. Quite worrying dreams. Very worrying dreams. For example, I had a dream about parrots the other night.
A: Parrots?
B: Yes. Green parrots. I mean, they shouldn't have been there because it, we weren't in any tropical country or anything.
A: Er. No. No.
B: It was a flock of parrots.
A: A flock?
B: A flock. A whole flock of parrots.
A: That's funny.
B: And there I was climbing up this stream bed ...
A: Yes. Um.
B: With these parrots flying around. Ha. Most extraordinary.
A: Really. Yes. Would you describe that as a nightmare?
B: Well it's rather worrying. Don't you think?
A: Very—Well, um, another question sir. How much time do you spend making your bed every day?
B: I don't spend any time at all. I just get out and then I get back in, in the evening.
A: I see. So no time at all. And, um. Yes the last question, um have you had any people complaining about your sleeping habits?
B: Complaining?
A: Yes. That's to say ...
B: What would they complain of?
A: D'you, perhaps you snore at night?
B: No I don't snore.
A: Perhaps you, you talk in your sleep.

B: No, I, I tend to take up rather a lot of room though.
A: Yes. I can see that.
B: Yes. Yes. I do tend to use up more than my fair share of the bed, yes.
A: But you ...
B: Roll around a bit.
A: But you've had no complaints?
B: Well, I occasionally get complaints but I don't take much notice of them. What can you do?
A: Yes. Quite so. Well um, thank you very much indeed sir. You've been very co-operative and helpful.
B: Yes. Well thank you. Yes. It was quite interesting speaking to you actually. Ha. Ha.
A: Goodbye.
B: Byebye.

Task d

Lian: This is Lian, and, like many of our listeners out there, I'm tired. I'm tired in the morning, I'm tired in the afternoon, and I'm really tired at night. And Frankly, I'm tired of being tired. My excuse is that I have two small children who sleep a little, and wake up a lot. Dr. Walsleben, why are we all so tired?

Dr. Walsleben: We're probably tired because we don't make sleep a priority. And I think as a young mother and a career woman, your days are pretty well filled, and I would suspect that you probably think you can do without sleep or at least cut your sleep short, and one of the things that happens is that we forget that sleep loss accumulates, so even one bad night, teamed with another will make an effect on our performance the following day. The other aspect, which you did touch on, is that even though we may sleep long periods of time, the sleep may not be really of good quality.

Lian: How serious of a problem is sleep deprivation?

Dr. Walsleben: Well, it can be very serious, because lack of sleep can affect our performance. It's not ... we can get cranky and all that, but if our performance is poor, and we are in a very critical job, we can have a major incident. And there have been many across society in which sleep and fatigue were issues.

The Exxon Valdez was one in which the captain got a lot of

	attention, but the mate who was driving the ship had been on duty for 36 hours. But you can read your local papers; every weekend, you'll see a car crash with probably a single driver at around 2 or 3 a.m., no reason why they would happen to drive off the road, and we all believe that that's probably a short sleep event that occurred when they weren't looking for it.
Lian:	Dr. Walsleben, I know how this sleep deprivation affects me. By the end of the day, with my children, I'm tired and cranky. I'm not making good parenting decisions. I don't have a lot to give my husband when he comes home, and then I just feel too tired to exercise. So I think, " Oh, I'll eat or I'll have a big cup of coffee, and that will give me the energy that I don't have naturally. Are these pretty common effects of sleep deprivation amongst your patients?"
Dr. Walsleben:	They're very common, and so many people accept them.
Lian:	I would even say that by Friday afternoon, I'm tired to get behind the wheel of a car, because I just feel like I am not a safe driver on the road. That's how tired I am by Fridays.
Dr. Walsleben:	I think it's great of you to have recognized that ... and that's a real, major concern for most America's workers. By Friday, everyone seems to be missing, probably, 5 hours of sleep.

Listening Two

Task a

(Steve)	
Miriam:	Yeah, when, when did you start smoking?
Steve:	Well, I started when I was, er, about sixteen, and I really started because I ... well, I think my family smoked and that really made me want to, er, ... really; somehow it was like growing up.
Miriam:	Yeah.
Steve:	And, of course, my friends around me were smoking and when we, when we left school we'd go over the park and have a s..., and have a quick cigarette. And, er, I mean, I do remember when I first started that I didn't really draw cigarettes at all because I didn't really know how to do it and I didn't think it was very pleasant; and it's only as time goes by you get

more and more involved in that, erm, in that process until finally you've ... you realise that you, you can't give up. And, in fact, when I first started I used to pretend that I was so hooked that I couldn't give up, because it was like being a child—it was like being a, being a grown-up. You know, grown-ups say they can't give up smoking, they wish they couldn't smoke and I used to pretend to say that. And of course, by the time it really happens it's too late. It doesn't mean the same thing any more. You actually want to give up but you can't.

(Miriam)

Miriam: I've smoked since I was eighteen and I started, er ... as you did, sort of ... sort of socially. And it wasn't a lot of fun to start with.

Steve: Right.

Miriam: It was quite embarrassing, sometimes, you know. You get smoke in your eyes and your eyes would water and it's a dead give-away that you've only just started.

Steve: Mmm.

Miriam: Er. And I didn't care for the taste all that much but everybody ... people smoked ... I mean I started smoking a long time ago before anything was known about cancer and, er ... it was just the thing to do. And as, as you said, it was a pa ..., it was being grown-up. It was drawing that line, you know: I am now grown up.

(Anne)

Anne: I should think I started at nine ... I started. No, I really started my first year at university. Everybody else smoked. It was just the thing to do. And now not so many people smoke, it's ... it seems to me that it was an awful waste of time and money. But my father smoked and my mother didn't so it was always a split thing in the house. I don't know, I really ... I think it probably just was a social habit more than anything else.

(John)

John: Like most people, I started smoking at school, foolishly. Er, I was offered cigarettes by other, er, children and in those days, I suppose smoking was the equivalent of drug-taking today; er, that it was considered, erm, ... erm ... fashionable and sophisticated and adult to smoke.

Recording Script

Task b

1. (Mike and Liz)

Mike: Have you ever tried?

Liz: Yes I ... I gave up, er, nearly two years ago now, um.

Mike: Have you found it difficult?

Liz: It wasn't too bad actually. Part of the reason I gave up was because I was pregnant, which is going to be difficult for you.

Mike: Yes, I'm not ... I'm not pregnant.

Liz: Um ... I found, er ... one of the easy things about it was I gave up drinking at the same time so ... er ... I always used to have a cigarette with a drink. So ... er ... it was, the actual smoking bit was relatively easy to stop.

Mike: I'm not sure I could withdraw both major props of my life at once.

Liz: No. That's ... that's quite tough.

2. (Miriam)

Miriam: I ... I once thought I wanted to give it up and this was before the cancer thing. Er ... because ... er, cigarettes went up from ... God ... something like one and nine to two shillings. Er ... and ... er ... so I thought "Oh this is a stupid waste of money, I'll give up smoking." And I gave up smoking for, I don't know, some weeks and I took up eating ... er ... and I, for some reason I took up eating apples. Apples weren't that cheap. I used to get through a couple of pounds of apples a day, and ... erm ... I was spending more on the bloody apples than I was on the smoking, and so I thought "Blow that!" So I ... er ... went back to ... back to smoking; but that was before the cancer thing.

3. (Alison)

Alison: Well, I always used to try and give up around New Year, because after the sort of Christmas festivities I usually had something like laryngitis or flu or a sore throat and it was a good time to give up 'cos I'd just smoked too much over Christmas. I just decided one New Year: that was it, I wasn't going to smoke any more, and I didn't.

4. (Christopher and Anne)

Christopher: Why was your third attempt successful, do you think?

Anne: Well, the third attempt was successful because I was pregnant, and so really smoking gave me up rather than me give up smoking. And I had no desire to go back to it once I had a small baby. But the times before it had been very difficult.

5. (Muriel)

Muriel: 'Cos that's the thing when I gave up the first time, it was ... I gave up because I had a really nasty taste in my mouth, and I just completely went off the idea of smoking and so I actually found it quite easy for the first year or so. I just didn't want a cigarette at all.

6. (Muriel and Cecil)

Cecil: I think that the ... for me ... erm ... the, the biggest incentive to try and give up again—as I say I've been trying to give up for twenty years now—is to take up some form of sport where smoking does make it more painful, so if I ... I notice that when I ...

Muriel: You've got to do an awful lot of sport, though ...

Cecil: No ...

Muriel: To reach the ...

Cecil: Well ... I noticed that about three years ago, when I used to play squash a lot, I realised that, you know, that smoking and squash didn't go together, and so then I gave up for some months; and, you know, I think that perhaps rather than try to give something up is take something else on.

7. (Miriam)

Miriam: I think perhaps the only thing that could really make me give up smoking would be to be in love with some ... with a non-smoker. Er ... who, you know, if it was a case of carrying on smoking and not being kissed, I'm not sure which would win.

Unit 7　Clubs/Societies

Listening One

Task b

Sally: ... so if you need any help with accommodation, please come and see me in

Recording Script

	room B302—that's in the basement.
Tim:	Thank you, Sally. Now, I know that all of you are wondering about all the different clubs and societies we have here, so I've asked some of the society presidents to say a few words about their clubs. First, um, yes, Kate, would you like to start?
Kate:	Uh, yes, thanks, Tim. Right. Well, I'd like to tell you something about the video club. It's one of the most popular clubs in the college; We have about 80 members at the moment. The club is one of the oldest in the college; in fact it began in 1981. I've been a member for two years and I've been the President since January. Um, we do three things really; our main job is to rent films on video and show these in the Student Common Room—that's on Tuesday and Friday evenings at eight o'clock. Then we also make our own video films. We've got two portable cameras, two studio cameras, an editing suite and a TV studio, so we can achieve quite professional results. And, in addition, we make a short magazine-type program each week. It's about ten minutes long and we show it just before the films on Tuesday and Friday evenings. Just very simple things: College sports results, um, any college news, things like that. Of course, membership of the club is completely free, and our members can use all the equipment as often as they like to make their own films. But you do have to pay for the video tape! So lastly, if anyone is interested in joining, please come and see me in the studio any time this week.
Tim:	OK. Thanks, Kate. Now, uh, Steve, could you say something about the football club?
Steve:	Yeah, thanks, Tim. Right, the football club ... um the first thing is the ...

Task c

Chairman:	Well, everyone, we've arranged this meeting so that some of the heads of our college societies can introduce themselves and their clubs to you, and give all of you who are new to the college an idea of the range of activities that are open to you. Who'd like to start? Yes, er, Roger Brown.
Roger:	Thank you. Well, my society is called the Historical Society, and as the name implies we were set up to provide a meeting place for all those among you who are interested in historical subjects. We meet every other Thursday in the Junior Common Room on F staircase

	and everybody is welcome. I think I should point out that we are not just interested in sitting around and talking about the past—a lot of our activity is directed towards what I can, perhaps, call "living history"—by which I mean history as it affects us now. And because of this we have in the past been very interested in exploring the history of this town itself—and some of its famous former inhabitants. We've also visited several historical houses in the area. This year we're planning on going out much more from the college to various historical sights and locations in a attempt to put history into perspective. So, do come and see me if you'd like to join—
Chairman:	Thanks, Roger. Now, I see Sharon is keen to speak—go ahead Sharon.
Sharon:	Thanks. Well I'm in charge of the Pop Music Society—although I suppose it should really be called the "Pop, rock, society" because we're really interested in all types of modern popular music and what we're into is helping to spread the knowledge and awareness of all types of modern music in whatever way we can. We hold meetings on Friday evenings in the stereo room to listen to new discs and talk about current trends. But over the years we've built up quite a large library of LPs, cassettes and more recently videos which we lend out at a small charge. In the past three or four years we've organized several concerts here at the college by a variety of local and interesting bands, but one of the things I'd like to do now I'm in charge is to increase the number of bands we can attract from different parts of the country. I'd also like to organize more bookings to big concerts at the major venues in London, Birmingham and Manchester. But to do that we need money—so I hope a lot of you will join the society and get behind us!
Chairman:	Thanks, Sharon. Now, Vanessa.
Vanessa:	Well, I'm one of the people in charge of running the college Drama Society—the Players. We attempt with what little resources we have to put on one play a term, and meeting to rehearse in the large assembly room in F block as often as possible, performing at the college theatre in the main buildings. I suppose our main objective is ... is that really—to put plays on and give everyone a chance to join in and enjoy the really super excitement of preparing and taking

Recording Script

	part in a play. We've done Schiller's *Wallenstein* and Strindberg's *To Damascus* in recent years—before my time I'm afraid. And this coming year we want to come more up to date and present plays by living authors and we'd be very interested if anyone at the college had a play they'd written that they would like us to do. We also have arranged visits to the theatre for the college and visits from several professional actors who have come down to talk to us about their fantastic jobs—and we've got more of those planned. So do come and join us—and get into Drama!
Chairman:	Thank you, Vanessa—now, I think Gibert wants to tell us a few words about the rowing club ... So, go ahead ...

Listening Two

Task b

A:	... So, I'll hand now to Julie Brooks.
B:	Thank you. Welcome to the Sports Center. It's good to see that there are so many people wanting to find out about our sports facilities.

First of all, membership. All students at the college are entitled to become members of the Sports Center, for an annual fee of £9.50. To register with us and get your membership card, you need to come to reception, between 2 and 6 p.m., Monday to Thursday. I'm afraid we can't register new members on Friday, so it's Monday to Thursday, 2 to 6, at reception. Now, there are three things that you must remember to bring with you when you come to register; they are: your Union card, a recent passport-sized photograph of yourself and the fee. It doesn't matter whether you bring cash or a cheque. We can't issue your card unless you bring all three; so, don't forget: your Union card, passport photo and fee.

Then once you have got your sports card, you will need to bring it with you whenever you come to book or use any Sports Center facilities. Booking over the phone is not allowed, so you have to come here in person, with your card, when you want to book. Our opening hours seem to get longer every year. We are now open from 9 a.m. to 10 p.m. on weekdays and from 10 a.m. to 6 p.m. on Saturdays.

For those of you who are up and about early in the morning, we are introducing a 50 percent "morning discount" this year. This is because the facilities tend to be under-used in the mornings last year. It means that all the sessions will be half-price between 9 a.m. and 12 noon on weekdays.

So, what exactly are the facilities? What sports can you play here? Well, this room we are in at the moment is called the Main Hall, and it's used mainly for team sports such as football, volleyball and basketball, but also for badminton and aerobics. On the other side of the reception area there is the dance studio; this provides a smaller, more intimate space, which we use for ballet, modern dance and martial arts—not at the same time, of course. Then in a separate building, which you may have noticed on your way here ... it's on the other side of the car park ... there are the squash courts (six of them), and at the far end of the building a fitness room. This is our newest facility, only completed in the spring, but it is already proving to be one of the most popular. As well as all these facilities available here on the campus, we also have an arrangement with the local tennis club, which is only two miles away, entitling our students to use their courts on weekday mornings in the summer.

So, I think that there should be something here for everybody, and I hope to see all of you at the Center, making use of the facilities. If, in the course of the year, you have any suggestions as to how the service we provide might be improved or its appeal widened, I'll be interested to hear from you.

Unit 8 Past Schooling

Listening One

Task b

Presenter: In this edition of our series "Children of a Decade" I'll be talking to Jack Thompson, who was born in 1940, and to Shirley Sutton, who was born in 1930. First of all, Jack, thanks for joining us. Perhaps ...

Jack: Not at all.

Presenter: Perhaps you'd tell us about your memories of your first holiday away from home?

Jack: Oh ... yes ... um ... at age ten I think it was, yes, I went to stay with an aunt at the seaside. Well, it wasn't a very happy experience. I felt very homesick at first.

Presenter: Mmm. And what about your first day at school, can you remember that?

Jack: Yes, I can. Er ... er ... I was five years old and I wanted to take all my toys with me but ... er ... they wouldn't let me. In the end it was agreed that I

Recording Script

	could take my teddy ... er ... but only on the first day.
Presenter:	Oh, I see. Your school days, were they happy ones?
Jack:	Well ... er ... I didn't have a very good time at school—I wasn't very bright, you see. And the teachers didn't seem to like me, but ... er ... I made a lot of friends and some of them I still keep in touch with. One of them I married.
Presenter:	Oh, that's wonderful. Well, did you have a favourite teacher?
Jack:	Miss Robinson ... or was it ... no, it was Miss Robson. My first teacher, that's right yeah ... very kind. Marvellous storyteller.
Presenter:	And who was your worst teacher?
Jack:	Mr. Goodman, that's right. We used to call him "Goody". Yeah, he pulled your ear if you made a mistake or talked in class. Yeah, my left ear is still bigger, look.
Presenter:	Ha ha. Perhaps you can tell us about your last day at school?
Jack:	My last day, oh yeah, that's emblazoned on my mind. Oh, I wanted to get my own back you see on old Mr. Goodman—the chap we used to call ... er ... "Goody"—so I put this bucket of water over the classroom door but it fell on him and he got soaked, you see. Ha ha. I've never seen anyone so angry. Oh, it was a good one, that.
Presenter:	Thank you very much, Jack. And now Shirley.
Shirley:	Yes.
Presenter:	Now, can you tell me about your first holiday away from home?
Shirley:	Oh yes ... er ... yes ... er ... at the age of eight it was. We went on holiday to the Lake District. We stayed at a little guest house, just me and my parents. Er ... I remember we had ... er ... honey for breakfast with ... er ... the toast and ... oh ... and porridge—I hated it.
Presenter:	That sounds lovely—oh, porridge, you hated it?
Shirley:	Ha ha.
Presenter:	Well, what about your first day at school?
Shirley:	Well, I ... I ... I don't remember any special incidents ... er ... Oh, I was very frightened and shy at first ... er ... I ... I know that, I can remember, but I soon came to enjoy school.
Presenter:	So your school days, were they happy?
Shirley:	Oh yes, I loved school! Oh, I was sorry when half-term came and ... and when the holidays came. Oh, perhaps this was because I was a bit of a goody-goody.

Presenter:	And what about your teachers? Did you have a favourite?
Shirley:	I did, yes. I remember her well. She was called Miss Brown and she was our history teacher. Oh, she really made history come to life—she really did.
Presenter:	Were there any bad moments? Did you have a worst teacher?
Shirley:	Aye, I did and I can remember her name too. Her name was Mrs. Sharpe and she taught maths. Oh, she had no patience. I wasn't all that good at maths and she always said to me. "You stupid girl!" It put me off maths for life.
Presenter:	Oh, what a shame.
Shirley:	I know.
Presenter:	Perhaps you could tell me about your last day at school?
Shirley:	Oh Yes, well, I'm afraid I cried. We sang our favourite hymn at the end of the term and I cried. It brought the tears to my eyes.
Presenter:	Oh, and it's bringing a tear to my eye now. Thank you very much.
Shirley:	Thank you.
Presenter:	And thank you too, Jack Thompson, thank you very much. Next week we'll be hearing from two people who were born in 1920 and 1910. So from me, Libby Freeman, goodbye.

Task d

Grace:	It's so great seeing you guys again.
Curtis:	Yeah.
Martin:	I agree.
Grace:	I can't believe it's been twenty years since we were all in college together.
Martin:	You know something, I remember it as if it were yesterday.
Curtis:	I do ... I was just going to say, as if it were yesterday.
Martin:	Incredible.
Grace:	Martin, what do you remember most about our college days?
Martin:	Oh, I remember most?
Grace:	Uh-huh.
Martin:	Curtis's hair ... down to his waist.
Curtis:	Now I remember how Grace looked. She always had a flower painted on her face. Remember that?
Martin:	Oh, yes. I remember that.
Grace:	Now wait, wait. Let's not forget about Martin and his air-conditioned blue

Recording Script

	jeans. I never saw anybody with more holes in their jeans than Martin.
Martin:	They're classic. You know, I still have those blue jeans.
Grace:	Still have them? I don't believe it.
Curtis:	Oh, incredible. I don't either.
Martin:	And I still wear them, too.
Curtis:	You know, I was thinking the other day—it's funny—about that worst ... worst thing happened in college.
Martin:	The worst thing?
Grace:	What was that?
Curtis:	Yeah. The time we were driving home from college for a spring break, remember? It was a holiday, and every gas station was closed. And the darn gas gauge was on empty.
Martin:	And (We were desperate.) we stopped at that gas station and tried to get some gas out of that pump.
Grace:	And the neighbors saw us and called the police. We almost got arrested. Gosh, I was scared stiff.
Martin:	You were scared stiff? I was petrified. And—but, you know, it was a lot different from the time we actually did get arrested.
Curtis:	Umm.
Grace:	Yeah. You know, that's my best memory. That peace demonstration. You know, somehow getting arrested for something you believe in isn't ... isn't scary at all.
Curtis:	No, it isn't at all.
Martin:	You're right.
Curtis:	But it did help that there were five hundred other students getting arrested along with us.
Martin:	That's true.
Grace:	I guess so.
Curtis:	That was a great day, though.
Grace:	Hey, hey, you all remember our last day of college?
Martin:	What, you mean graduation?
Curtis:	Graduation, what's to remember? None of you went to graduation. I didn't go.
Martin:	Do you regret that, that ... that after all these years you skipped out on the ceremony?
Grace:	Not me. Hey, I've changed my mind about a lot of things in twenty years,

	but I don't think we missed anything that day.
Curtis:	No, nothing at all. And that picnic that the three of us had by the stream, remember? (That was great.) Drinking wine, playing guitar, singing. Oh, that was worth more to me than any graduation ceremony.
Martin:	That was the best graduation ceremony there could have been.
Curtis:	Mm.

Listening Two

Task a

Angela:	Can you remember your first day at school, William? I can't remember mine.
William:	Vaguely—I can remember not knowing whether to laugh or cry because I was so upset at spending ... at leaving my family and going away from my mother and father.
Brenda:	Was it a boarding school?
William:	It wasn't, it was a day school, but up until then I'd spent, you know, all time ... all the time at home.
Brenda:	This was when you were little.
William:	Yes, when I was about seven, six or seven. But I was also very happy because I had a uniform for the first time in my life and I had a hat, particularly the hat I remember ...
Angela:	Oh, how sweet ...
William:	... I loved that and I used to wear it for about a week before I went to school. When I actually got to school, I was very uneasy and refused to sit down and actually went round the class knocking all the other kids onto the floor and only then could I sit down.
Brenda:	Gosh! What a ...
Angela:	Very difficult ...
William:	... which is a rather strange thing to do, which I don't actually remember, but it was reported to my mother and she told me, years later.
Brenda:	Did they forgive you, did the children forgive you? Did you make friends?
William:	I suppose so. I don't remember being kind of, er, particularly unpopular because of it, but maybe I was.

Recording Script

Brenda: I can remember my secondary school, I can remember ... It had a very long avenue of trees and I remember walking up that long avenue of trees in my new uniform with my new hat and my new satchel and I was very, very frightened, but later on when I'd been at the school for some time I grew to really love that avenue of trees.

Angela: But I wonder if you like teachers in relation to the subjects that you like. I mean, are your favourite teachers the teachers of your favourite subjects?

Brenda: No, mine weren't, no, because my favourite subject was history and that was taught ... I can't even remember her name ... She was a very, very old-fashioned, quite old, rather thin woman with grey hair and not very kind, but she was just a very, very good teacher. She really made the subject come alive, and she was passionate about the subject herself and that made it really interesting for the rest of us.

William: But there were teachers you liked because they made the subject interesting, and you liked the subject, whether it was history or English or whatever, and there were other teachers that were quite good fun, but ... just because you could, kind of, have ... poke fun at them and ... muck around during the class.

Brenda: Yes, because they were nice personalities.

William: Yes, but you didn't actually learn that much.

Brenda: No, because I like my geography teacher, but I absolutely hated geography. I didn't like my French teacher and I adored French, so I mean it was ...

William: Yes.

Angela: I hated maths ...

Brenda: ... most people hated maths at school.

Angela: I was asked ... they asked me if I wanted to stop doing maths when I was fourteen because I was so bad at it and that teacher was called ... She was very fat and very horrible and she was called Mrs. Hughes-Davies and we called her Hugs-Bugs.

William: Well, I don't think those things, er, you should think of them in terms of whether you can remember the information now, they teach you to, kind of, think, they teach you how to think, and that can be useful later on, um, just in terms of how you cope with things outside education.

Angela: Yes.

William: It's not just qualifications for getting a job.

Brenda:	Oh, it is now though. I think qualifications now are fantastically important, much more important than they were when we were young.
Angela:	That's right, I agree.
Brenda:	Because there are so few, you know, there are fewer jobs.
Angela:	Well I agree they're important because jobs are important, but I don't think the answer to that is to make education entirely geared towards qualifications. The answer is to create more jobs, um, because I think education's much more useful as a general training of how to think about things, how to analyse things.
Brenda:	But it used to be, when I was younger ...

Unit 9   Past and Future

Listening One

Task a

1. Simon: Well, I think it was my great grandfather who came over here back at the turn of the century. He came over here from Poland in about 1901, and after he had been here for about ten years he met my great grandmother—she had escaped from Russia with her parents. They'd been living in great poverty over there—and they got married in about 1910, I suppose.

2. Ronda: My family's only been over here about four generations—we're not part of the original "convict stock"! No, my great grandparents had been living in the south-west of England and they'd obviously been having a pretty hard time of it, so my old great grandpa ... he looked around and said "Australia's the place for us", I guess. Now originally when they came over, they settled in Melbourne, but my father, when he was a lad, he met my mother on a business trip when he was in Sydney and when they got married he upped and moved and we've been living here as a family ever since.

3. Alistair: Oh, for many generations, of course. I once looked into the old family tree and I found that we really can trace our ancestors back to one of the families that came over with William, the Conqueror. Yeah. But it was my grandparents who built the house. You see my grandfather had been living in the large old mansion for—oh many years—and the costs and the discomfort were

becoming just too much for him. So after he'd tried to find someone to buy it and just couldn't, well, he gave it to the nation, and had this rather more modest seventeen-bedroom house built, and we all moved into here in, I suppose 1926–1927 something like that and we've been living here ever since.

4. Caroline: I think in a way it's a bit of, well, you know, history repeating itself because, well, apparently my great grandmother also married a Frenchman. She'd been living over there with a cousin or something—in the South of France—and she met my great grandfather at a gala ball in the Casino—very romantic! But no ... I met Armand in the local supermarket actually! I'd been looking for some washing powder of all things and I'd spilt all the things I had in my basket and I was just bending down to pick them all up and I looked up ... and there was this most gorgeous man!

Listening Two

Task a

Man:	Hi.
Woman:	Hi.
Man:	What'd you do last night?
Woman:	I watched TV. There was a really good movie called *Soylent Green*.
Man:	*Soylent Green*?
Woman:	Yeah. Charlton Heston was in it.
Man:	What's it about?
Woman:	Oh, it's about life in New York in the year 2022.
Man:	I wonder if New York will still be here in the year 2022.
Woman:	In this movie, in 2022 ...
Man:	Yeah?
Woman:	... New York has forty million people.
Man:	Ouch!
Woman:	And twenty million of them are unemployed.
Man:	How many people live in New York now? About seven or eight million?
Woman:	Yeah, I think that's right.
Man:	Mm-hmm. You know, if it's hard enough to find an apartment now in New York City, what's it going to be like in 2022?
Woman:	Well, in this movie most people have no apartment. So thousands sleep on

	the steps of buildings. People who do have a place to live have to crawl over sleeping people to get inside. And there are shortages of everything. The soil is so polluted that nothing will grow. And the air is so polluted they never see the sun. It's really awful.
Man:	I think I'm going to avoid going to New York City in the year 2022.
Woman:	And there was this scene where the star, Charlton Heston, goes into a house where some rich people live.
Man:	Hu-huh.
Woman:	He can't believe it, because they have running water and they have soap.
Man:	Really?
Woman:	And then he goes into the kitchen and they have tomatoes and lettuce and beef. He almost cries because he's never seen real food in his life, you know, especially the beef. It was amazing for him.
Man:	Well, if most people have no real food, what do they eat?
Woman:	They eat something called soylent.
Man:	Soylent?
Woman:	Yeah. There's soylent red and soylent yellow and soylent green. The first two are made out of soy-beans. But the soylent green is made out of ocean plants. The people eat it like crackers. That's all they have to eat.
Man:	That sounds disgusting.
Woman:	Well, you know, it really isn't that far from reality.
Man:	No?
Woman:	Yeah. Because, you know the greenhouse effect that's beginning now and heating up the earth ...
Man:	Oh, yeah, I've heard about that.
Woman:	... because we're putting the pollutants in the atmosphere, you know?
Man:	Mm-hmm.
Woman:	I mean, in this movie New York has ninety-degree weather all year long. And it could really happen. Uh ... like now, we ... we have fuel shortages. And in the movie there's so little electricity that people have to ride bicycles to make it.
Man:	You know something? I don't think that movie is a true prediction of the future.
Woman:	I don't know. It scares me. I think it might be.
Man:	Really?
Woman:	Well, yeah.

Task d

Interviewer: It's a well known science fiction plot to freeze a body and bring it back to life years later. However, this may no longer be so far from the truth. Joining us from our Cardiff studio is Professor Andrew Morgan, who's been doing some research into this subject. Professor Morgan.

Professor Morgan: Yes, well, I've been looking into the er ... the ability of certain animals to freeze themselves for a certain amount of time, and then to come back to life when the circumstances around them change. And, what I've been working on over the past two years is the particular process that enables them to do this.

Interviewer: What have you actually discovered?

Professor Morgan: I think it's a particular chemical in the animals' bodies which begins to work under certain circumstances. And I'm now experimenting with this chemical to see if I can get other animals who wouldn't normally be able to freeze themselves to be able to do this.

Interviewer: Have you had any success?

Professor Morgan: I have so far. It's been going very well. And I'm reasonably confident that erm ... well, perhaps within ten years from now I'll be able to freeze human beings for as long or as short a time as I would like to, and then bring them back to life again in exactly the same state that they were in before they were frozen ... just as you can do with animals.

Interviewer: And what's the main application of your research?

Professor Morgan: I think the main application of this for human beings would be to ... for people with terminal illnesses, people who have got illnesses which cannot be cured at the moment. We could freeze them, find a cure for the illness and then bring them back to life again and administer the cure.

Interviewer: I see. Erm ... these people could actually choose to prolong their lives and therefore not suffer ...

Professor Morgan: Yes, I think so. Somebody suffering from, say, multiple sclerosis, certain types of cancer, of course, AIDS would be another particular disease ... People would be able to choose to have

	their lives, er ... frozen at that particular moment and then brought back to life when a cure appeared.
Interviewer:	Well, this obviously is going to create great ... er great debate I would think as to the rights and wrongs of whether we should be actually doing this.

Unit 10　Commercials/Advertisements

Listening One

Task a

Ad. 1

Announcer:	You pack your car, and your worst nightmare happens! When you come back ... it's gone! It can happen anywhere ... and chances are, one day, it will happen to you! That's why you need the incredible Thief Buster security system. It's easy to use and 100 percent effective. If someone so much as touches your car, an alarm will ring. And if that doesn't stop the thief, the engine will turn off when he tries to start the car. So why put your car at risk any longer? Get a Thief Buster security system today! Thief Buster ... protection for your piece of mind!

Ad. 2

Brad:	Hello?
Lisa:	Hi, Brad! It's Lisa. How was your job interview?
Brad:	It was terrible! I was wearing that dark blue jacket ... you know ... the one with the gold buttons ...
Lisa:	Uh-huh?
Brad:	Well, I noticed that the boss kept looking at my shoulders. I couldn't figure it out, so I took a quick look and saw all these white, powdery flakes.
Lisa:	From your head?
Brad:	Yeah, it was dandruff! You could really see it too ... because of the jacket. It was so embarrassing ... and it totally threw me off. I just

	couldn't concentrate on the questions.
Announcer:	Dandruff can be a small problem with big consequences. Luckily there's Rinse Away dandruff shampoo to take care of even your toughest dandruff. Don't let the embarrassment of an itchy, flaky scalp show you down. Just Rinse Away and feel the confidence. Rinse Away—your sure cure for dandruff!

Task b

The Goodhayes Advertising Agency are developing the image for a new product that they are working on. Listen to part of their committee meeting.

Chairman:	Now, ladies and gentlemen, you all know why we're meeting this afternoon. We want to decide on a definite advertising campaign for the new product we've received from ... Tony, I know you want to say something.
Tony:	Yes, thank you, Mr. Chairman. As I've said this is not something that people will want to buy; there are similar products on the market and we need to work out the advertisements very carefully, or we won't sell any at all.
Chairman:	I'm more hopeful, but I agree that we'll have to sell this through good advertising and attractive packaging. Linda, you've got examples of the packaging ideas with you, haven't you?
Linda:	Yes, here you are. We tried two different styles: there's a can, like this; or a bottle, like this. We preferred the bottle, because it looks so clean and clear. What do you think?
George:	Well, I like the can. It's more modern and I think it will appeal more to young people as they're used to drinks in cans. And all our competitors put their drinks in bottles.
Tony:	I agree. We've got to be different. A pure white can, with the name "Clensip" in blue. That's good.
Lucy:	We ought to decide what is special and new and different.
Tony:	There isn't anything new about it, except the can. That's what's going to make it so hard to sell.
Linda:	I don't agree with you. It's a good product. It's healthy, it's pure, it's natural, it's good for you.
Chairman:	Yes, that's the idea. We want to sell it to the people because it's healthy.
Lucy:	Can we say "It's Clensip, naturally it's good for you."

Tony:	I like that—that means "Of course, it's good for you"; it also means that it's natural.
George:	Yes, that's OK. But I thought we wanted to be different. All the other brands advertise how healthy and pure they are.
Linda:	Well, there's no alternative. People will buy this because it's pure. It's the only reason for buying it. What else can you say?
Lucy:	It isn't fattening, I suppose?
Chairman:	"Drink Clensip, the non-fattening drink in a can." We could have a picture—a beautiful, slim young lady drinking a can of Clensip. Yes, that's a good idea.
Tony:	Yes, it's quite unusual to drink it by itself, without adding anything.
George:	We could say "Be different—drink Clensip."
Lucy:	The beautiful girl ought to be different, too. Perhaps we could have a lot of girls all wearing red dresses, and one girl, in a white dress, who's drinking Clensip.
Tony:	We want everyone to drink Clensip, not just girls. Perhaps we could have a lot of young men in little sailing boats, and then one young man in a white suit, sailing a big yacht, and drinking Clensip.
Chairman:	I think we could have a whole series of those pictures. Any other ideas?
George:	People think of it as a drink. What about adding it to different things? You could wash your hair in it, for instance.
Chairman:	In Clensip?
George:	Why not? People wash their hair in beer, sometimes.
Lucy:	Clensip wouldn't hurt your hair. In fact, it would be …
George:	What about: "A Clensip Beauty Book"?
Linda:	Wash your face in Clensip?
Tony:	Clean your teeth in Clensip after every meal.
Chairman:	I think we've got something here. Let's see. How many words can you think of to describe Clensip? We've got pure, natural, clear, clean, healthy.
Lucy:	Refreshing.
Linda:	Soothing—soak your tired feet in Clensip.
George:	Sparkling—bathe your eyes in sparkling Clensip.
Tony:	How about: "Freshen up your floors with Clensip?"
Lucy:	Add Clensip to your cooking …, making ice-cream …

Recording Script

Listening Two

Task a

Waverley—a holiday you'll never forget.

Anthony went to see his boss, Simon, to discuss his problem.

Anthony: Look here, I can't possibly do this.

Simon: What is it, Tony? Problems?

Anthony: Have you seen what's turned up on my desk? Look at this!

Simon: Let's see: "The Waverley Hotel is one of the finest tourist hotels on the west coast of England. It is set in wonderful countryside and offers first class comfort and service ..." Well, what's wrong with that? It seems all right to me.

Anthony: What's wrong with it? It's a pack of lies—that's what's wrong with it. Do you remember when I went on holiday last year?

Simon: Oh, yes, yes, and you ended up at that terrible hotel ...

Anthony: That's right. This was the hotel.

Simon: The Waverley?

Anthony: The Waverley.

Simon: What was wrong with it exactly?

Anthony: Everything was wrong with it! The room was dark; the walls were damp; the bed was lumpy; the food was terrible and the beer was flat. Dinner was always late; breakfast was always burnt, and lunch was always cold. The staff were rude and unhelpful. And it was terribly expensive.

Simon: You didn't like it.

Anthony: I didn't like it. And I really don't feel that I can stand there and tell the world that it's a wonderful hotel.

Simon: Well, no one will know that it's your voice. You don't appear on the film.

Anthony: That's not the point. The point is that I don't want to advertise this hotel when I know it's so terrible.

Simon: It might not be terrible now. It's a year since you went there. They may have changed a lot of things.

Anthony: They certainly should have done!

Simon: They've just been given a very good rating by the Tourist Board. They can't be all that bad.

Anthony: It says here "The hotel is very comfortable and convenient." It can't have changed all that much! If that sentence is true they must have

	pulled down the old hotel and built another one! There are laws about advertising.
Simon:	Of course there are, and this hotel is nothing like as bad as you make out. I'm sorry you had a rotten holiday.
Anthony:	I should've asked for my money back! Do you really expect me to stand there and read this, saying what a wonderful hotel it is?
Simon:	Yes, I do expect you to. The hotel has had a good rating. They've paid for a video film advertising their hotel, and you're going to provide it.
Anthony:	I'm not going to read this: "This hotel is extremely comfortable and convenient." They might think it is, but that's not the same thing.
Simon:	Well, change the words a bit, if it worries you that much. "This hotel prides itself on being comfortable and convenient." How does that sound?
Anthony:	It comes to the same thing.
Simon:	Except that you're offering the hotel's opinion, and not your own.
Anthony:	I still don't like it.
Simon:	You're not paid to like it.
Anthony:	Well, OK then, but only if I can go through the script and change it a bit.
Simon:	Oh, come on Tony. If I let you change the script, you'll ruin the advertisement, you know you will. I can't let you write your own version when you make it clear you heartily dislike the place.
Anthony:	Well, I promise to show it to you before I record it.
Simon:	Well ...
Anthony:	In fact, this could be rather fun!

Task b

The Waverley Hotel welcomes you to some of the most beautiful countryside in the South West, and the service it offers has to be seen to be believed. You stand at the elegant front door, and your first impression is of comfort and welcome. You glance into one of the two crowded restaurants, and see that the menu is excellent, and the tablecloths and silver quite clean. The standard of waiting is remarkable, and waiters are everywhere.

Here you will come to sample the fish, freshly caught in the nearby stream, and only just cooked. You may even enjoy the home-made pie, which is produced by the cook to a secret recipe. Nobody knows what the ingredients are. There are other Waverley specialities which you will have to eat. There is, for example, a long table of freshly-made desserts, creating a beautiful sight, and usually scent, right back to the kitchens.

Recording Script

You make your way to your room. Perhaps you have one of the large, comfortable rooms at the front of the house, overlooking the gardens. Or perhaps you have chosen one of the smaller rooms, but you can be comfortable in one of these. Remember, no bed is more comfortable than a Waverley bed. You will find the staff, who are there to answer your questions, polite and courteous, and should you require anything at any time, such as clean sheets or a hot cup of tea, you are very welcome to ask.

If you stay at the Waverley you will have a holiday which you will never forget, and at a price which will surprise you!

Unit 11   Entertainment

Listening One

Task a

Narrator: Three friends are discussing what movie to see. Fill in the missing information in the ads. Then complete the note to John.
Susan: What are we doing tonight?
Cindy: Don't you remember? (Hmm.) We decided to go to a movie.
Susan: What do you want to see?
Bob: Uh ... hey, is John coming with us?
Susan: Yes, if we go to a movie.
Bob: Well, what's playing?
Cindy: Well, why don't I check the paper? (Hey, good idea.) (Mm.) Um ... let's see ... Arts and Leisure Section ... um ... (Mm-hmm.) OK, here we go. (Uh-huh.) Westside Cinema—they're playing *Empire Strikes Back*, (Da-dum!) ugh, with showtimes at 7:10 and 9:45.
Bob: OK, what else is playing?
Cindy: Uh ... Circle Theater. There's *Rocky III*, (Mm.) 7:05 and 9:30.
Bob: I don't know about you, but I've kind of had it up to here with *Rocky*, but uh ... I kind of like *Empire Strikes Back*. You know, if we went to a later show, it'd give us time to eat first.
Susan: Oh, that sounds good.
Bob: How much does it cost?
Cindy: Uh ... let's see. *Empire* tickets ... five dollars ... mm ...

179

Susan: O-o-oh! (Yeah.) Well, I've seen *Empire Strikes Back* twice and I really don't feel like seeing that again. (Oh.) What's at the Palace?

Bob: Uh ... Palace. Palace. Isn't that that cheap theater with the small screen?

Susan: Yeah, (Aw.) but the tickets are only two-fifty. (Oh.)

Cindy: Hey, they're showing *Kramer versus Kramer* at eight o'clock.

Susan: Hey, (Mm.) that's a great movie! (I love that movie!) I hear that's a real tear jerker. (Oh, it is. Mm.)

Bob: What's ... what's at the Metro? What's on there?

Cindy: Uh ... *Casablanca* with Humphrey Bogart (Oh!) and Ingrid Bergman!

Bob: Great!

Cindy: There's a show at ten past nine. Tickets are four dollars.

Susan: Oh, I adore that movie. I never get tired of seeing it. (Mm.)

Cindy: You know, I'd like to see that. You know I've never seen it? Hey, we could meet John before the show at the Sunset Bar and Grill, (Oh, great!) across the street from the theater.

Bob: Oh, good. Let's go to the Sunset Bar, and I vote for *Casablanca*.

Cindy: Yeah, oh, Bob, I know—you just want to drink at the Sunset Bar.

Bob: No, no. I've always been a Bogart fan, you know?

Susan: Sounds good to me. Now, remember, the movie starts at ten after nine, and I think that we all ought to meet at the Sunset around eight o'clock. (Great.)

Cindy: That sounds good. Well, why don't I leave John a note telling him what we're going to do.

Susan: OK, tell John that if he can't make it to the Sunset, he should meet us outside the theater five minutes before the movie starts. (OK.) Oh, wait, wait, no. Make that ten minutes, in case there's a line.

Cindy: Oh, yeah! Good thinking! (Yeah, could be.) All right, why don't you two figure out whose car we're taking, and I'll write this note.

Task b

Rob: ... see a film tonight? There's a really good film on at the local cinema.

Susie: Oh, what one?

Rob: *Casablanca*.

Susie: Oh! Oh no, that's ages old, isn't it?

Rob: Yeah, but have you seen it?

Susie: No, I don't think, no ...

Rob:	Oh, it's fantastic, I mean it was made in the forties. It's wartime drama, but it's absolutely brilliant. It's got that old line "Play it again, Sam" ... it's fantastic!
Susie:	Mmm, no, I don't really feel like, I don't ... that's, that's too old, that, I mean I'd rather see something a bit more up to date, I mean ...
Rob:	What else is on?
Susie:	Well, er ...
Rob:	There's some old, oldish films on lately ...
Susie:	Oh, G .... *Rambo*'s on, oh dear ...
Rob:	Oh, I'm not going to see that ... I haven't seen it, but I mean I hate things like that.
Susie:	I just find that all, well, he's revolting ...
Rob:	Gratuitous violence, it's terrible.
Susie:	Ah, you know, I really think that you'd like this one, um ...
Rob:	What?
Susie:	... um, er, *Psycho*.
Rob:	I've seen it.
Susie:	Have you?
Rob:	Yeah. I mean, it's great ... it's great, but you don't want to see *Casablanca* because it's old—*Psycho*'s almost as old as that.
Susie:	Yeah, I know, but, I mean, it's a thriller, isn't it? I mean it's you know, it's ... oh, it's brilliant!
Rob:	It is a bit dated now, though, isn't it?
Susie:	Yeah, yeah, I supp ..., yeah, yeah, I mean, I don't mind what we see. I mean there isn't much choice really, I mean, it's all ... they're all pretty old, really ... most of the things that are on.
Rob:	I know exactly which film you'd like, but you may have seen it.
Susie:	What?
Rob:	*E.T.* Have you seen it?
Susie:	Yeah. Oh it's so sweet!
Rob:	I know. Even I almost cried in that.
Susie:	I know, it's a real tear-jerker.
Rob:	Well, we've both seen that, so there's not much point ...
Susie:	Yeah, there's no point in seeing that. *Chariots of Fire* looks pretty dull to me. Um ...
Rob:	Oh, I quite fancy that, actually.

Susie: Mmm, no ...

Rob: Excellent music.

Susie: True, true enough ...

Rob: Perhaps you'd be interested in seeing *The Sound of Music*!

Susie: I feel like seeing something quite, quite gory ... quite, kind of frightening in a way, um ...

Rob: There's nothing on like that ... there's only ... *Psycho* ...

Susie: What is there? *The Godfather*!

Rob: Oh yeah!

Susie: How about going to see *The Godfather*?

Rob: Yeah, OK. I love Brando.

Susie: Yeah, so do I. I mean that's old as well, but *Casablanca*'s a bit of a weepie, really.

Rob: Alright, let's go and see *The Godfather*.

Listening Two

Task b

Announcer: Good evening, and welcome to this evening's viewing on TV America International. Before we go on to our first program, let me tell you what we've chosen for you tonight.

Beginning in a few minutes' time at 7:05, is *Regional Special*; part of our documentary series which takes a look at some of the more traditional ways of living that still exist in many parts of our country. Today we'll be seeing the old Dutch communities in Pennsylvania.

After Regional Special, at 7:50 there is the *News*—a look at today's national and international news events. After that, at 8:10 you can settle down in your armchairs for episode sixteen of our extremely popular series *High Society*. This will be followed at 9:00 by a live variety show presenting such all time greats as Eric Clapton and Woody Allen as well as some more recent talent—that great rock band, Fusion. At 10:00 we have fifteen minutes of *Cleaver the Cat* cartoons, and at 10:15 our sports program, highlighting all today's important national and international sporting events.

And then at 11:00 you can see our late night news. At 11:15 we come to our popular health program *Keeping Fit*. Tonight we will be looking at some of the dangers involved in keeping fit.

Recording Script

And last of all, at midnight, we have our midnight movie which tonight features Dustin Hoffman in his light-hearted but serious comedy *Tootsie*.

Well, that's what we've planned for your viewing this evening. We hope you enjoy our selection and may we wish you good viewing.

Unit 12 Climate and Weather

Listening One

Task b

Anchorwoman: ... and that's the Friday night news. Now over to Dave Spellman for the weekend weather forecast. Dave, what do you have in store for us this weekend?

Weatherman: Well, Linda, it's still raining here in Chicago, and it looks like that rain is going to continue through the weekend. It'll be cloudy tomorrow with scattered showers, and the outlook for Sunday—more rain and colder. The predicted high for tomorrow is forty-five degrees Fahrenheit, but the thermometer is expected to dip to the freezing point tomorrow night, with a temperature of thirty-two degrees. I'm afraid colder weather is on its way!

Let's take a look now at the weather across the country. Showers expected tomorrow down the West Coast as far south as San Francisco. Fair weather in the low seventies predicted for the Los Angeles area; fair in San Diego. There's a cold front from Canada moving down through the western states. Thirty-eight degrees in Denver, Colorado, with thirty-mile-an-hour winds, and it's expected to be cold and windy right through the weekend. Dallas is experiencing unseasonably cold weather—forty-eight degrees. It's raining as far east as Detroit and Toronto, and that rain is going to continue through tomorrow, when it may turn to snow. Currently forty-three degrees in Detroit, forty-one degrees in Toronto. And temperatures dropping.

It's snowing heavily in Montreal, ladies and gentlemen, its first storm of the season, and we expect that snow activity to move down from Canada into the eastern states sometime tomorrow, probably reaching the New York area sometime tomorrow night. Good weather across the south. Clear skies in Miami, and they're going to enjoy a sunny seventy-eight degrees in that town this weekend, so if you're thinking about a vacation, now's the time to do it. Back to Chicago. Once again, continuing rain tonight through Sunday. Current temperature, thirty-eight degrees. And that winds up our weather report for this evening. This is Dave Spellman. Have a good night, and if you're going out, don't forget your umbrella.

Task c

Announcer: ... and now over to the weather centre where Harry Spicer is going to tell you all about your holiday weather.

Weatherman: Thank you, Jenny. Yes, this is the first really busy holiday weekend coming up and I'll begin with some information about the weather in Europe and around the Mediterranean. Starting off, though, with England and Wales to give you an idea of the kind of weather those of us who are staying at home are going to get. Well, quite a warm day tomorrow with temperatures around 24 degrees mark and ... er ... hazy sunshine in most places. On the Continent, rather a different picture. In Scandinavia, Sweden can expect quite a cold day with temperatures of 15 degrees and some quite heavy rain in the east. Norway and Denmark less cold but still wet most of the day. In France, the high pressure may give rise to a shower here and there, especially in the west but over most of the country there'll be hazy sunshine and temperatures very similar to those in England and Wales, around 25 degrees Centigrade. Spain should be warm and dry with temperatures up to 30 degrees and a lot of sunshine and a similar picture in Italy, where it may get even hotter and temperatures around 33 degrees can be expected tomorrow. The very hot weather recently in the Eastern Mediterranean has been hitting the headlines but this seems to be over now and if you're going to Greece, you can expect some very heavy thunderstorms in the afternoon and evening: it's going to be quite a lot cooler than of late ... er ... temperatures round

Recording Script

about 25 degrees here tomorrow. Morocco and the rest of the southern Mediterranean is going to be extremely hot around 35 degrees but here it may well be quite cloudy during the day with skies not clearing until nightfall. Finally a big contrast in the Alps, where snow has been falling over the mountains in Switzerland and Austria since this morning. Here above 2,000 metres it'll be around freezing most of the day tomorrow and there'll be more snow, some of it quite heavy. So if you're headed in that direction, perhaps you'd better take your winter clothes.

That's all from me for now and ... er ... now back to Jenny.

Listening Two

Task a

Announcer: And now over to Marsha Davenport for today's weather forecast. Marsha?

Weather reporter: Thanks, Peter. Well, as you can see from the weather map, there's varied weather activity across the United States and Canada today. Let's start with the west coast, where it's raining from British Columbia down to northern California. The high in Seattle will be 50 degrees. Southern California will be in better shape today—they'll have sunny skies and warmer temperatures. We're looking for a high of 78 degrees in San Diego. The midwest will be having clear but windy weather. Oklahoma City will see a high of 65 and sunny skies, with very strong winds. Down in Houston we're looking for cloudy skies and a high of 69. Over to the east in Miami we expect the thermometer to reach 64 degrees, but it'll be cloudy and quite windy. Up in the northeast, it looks like winter just won't let go! New York City will be having another day of heavy rains, high winds, and cold temperatures, with a high of only 35 degrees expected. Further north in Montreal it's even colder—28 degrees, with snow flurries expected today. Over in Toronto it's sunny but a cold 30 degrees.

And that's this morning's weather forecast. We'll have a complete weather update today at noon.

Unit 13 Accommodation

Listening One

Task b

House agent:	... right, if you'd just come this way.
Woman:	Thank you.
Man:	Yes.
House agent:	Er ... on the right here we have the ... er ... the bathroom, which as you can see is fully ... fully fitted. If we just move forward now, we ... er ... come into the er ... main ... main bed-sitting room here. And ... er ... on the left are dining room table and chairs.
Woman:	Oh yes.
Man:	Yes.
House agent:	And er ... straight ahead of us ... um ... fold-away double bed and mattress, which I think you'll agree is quite a novel idea.
Man:	Oh yes.
House agent:	And then ... um ... to ...
Woman:	Behind the armchair.
House agent:	Yes, behind the armchair. To our right, um ... in the corner there, a fitted wardrobe. And another one on my left here.
Woman:	On either side of the bed?
House agent:	Yes, that's right. That's right, so you can put all your ... er ... night attire or what ... whatever you like in there.
Man:	Yes, that's good.
House agent:	Then, there ... the ... we have the sofa here ... er ... in front of the ... um ... the window.
Man:	Oh yes.
House agent:	Er ... so there's plenty of light coming through into the room and as you can see there's a nice view through the windows there.
Woman:	No curtains, though.
House agent:	No curtains, but we've got roller blinds.
Woman:	Oh.
House agent:	Yes, they're nice and straightforward. No problems about that—don't have to wash them of course. And ... um ... on the left of

	the ... er ... sofa there, you can see nice coffee tables ... er ... and ... matching with the coffee table of course in front of us.
Woman:	Oh yes, they're the same, aren't they?
House agent:	If ... if we move straight a ... straight ahead, actually, into the ... er ... the kitchen you can see that um ... on my left here we've got a washing machine, tumble dryer and ... um ... electric cooker ...
Woman:	Oh yes.
Man:	Mmm.
House agent:	All as you can see to the most modern designs. And there um ... on the other side of the kitchen ... um ... refrigerator there in the ... in the corner.
Man:	Oh yeah, yes.
Woman:	Oh, what a nice little cubbyhole! Yes, very neat.
House agent:	Yes. Well ... um ... I don't know whether you've got any questions. That's it, of course.
Woman:	Well, could ... could we perhaps see the bathroom, because we ... we didn't see that?
House agent:	OK, yes, yes. Let's go on out of here and ... um ... end up in the bathroom ...

Task c

(Listen to Mrs. Hunt and the agent, discussing the property.)

Estate Agent:	Well, here we are Mrs. Hunt. If I can just find the key we can go inside. There we are. Nice little entrance hall, with a telephone point.
Mrs. Hunt:	Mm, this is a nice, big room.
Estate Agent:	Yes, lovely, big windows. Very light and airy. A power point on the wall, over there.
Mrs. Hunt:	No central heating?
Estate Agent:	No, not at this price. Mind you, lots of people like a real fire in a room like this.
Mrs. Hunt:	Makes a lot of dust though, a real fire.
Estate Agent:	Well, it would be very easy to install central heating. It's an east-facing room, too. Gets all the morning sun. And through here is another big room. This one faces west, so you've always got a big window facing the sun.
Mrs. Hunt:	It's awfully dark in here at the moment. I don't like that wallpaper.

Estate Agent:	Well, you can always paint over it. Though it would be a pity, I think. The decoration everywhere is in excellent condition.
Mrs. Hunt:	If you like bright yellow, that is. And I'm afraid if I did paint over the wall-paper, the daffodils would still show through. What's through here?
Estate Agent:	This brings us back into the hall, and opposite is the kitchen. After you.
Mrs. Hunt:	Mm ... the kitchen's not bad.
Estate Agent:	Built-in cupboards, plenty of power points, modern sink-unit, nice, big windows and looking onto the garden.
Mrs. Hunt:	Not much of a garden, is it? All lawn like that. I like a few flowers, myself.
Estate Agent:	Keen on gardening, are you?
Mrs. Hunt:	Well, my husband used to be, but he's got a bad leg now, so he can't walk about much or do things like he used to.
Estate Agent:	Well, you don't want a garden which needs a lot of digging, then. A couple of climbing roses up that wall and you'd have no end of color.
Mrs. Hunt:	Yes, I quite like the kitchen. Apart from the color scheme, that is ... Oh, I don't know. It's all right, I suppose. What's in here? Ah, the dining-room.
Estate Agent:	Very handy, right next door to the kitchen. A bit smaller than the other two reception rooms, but a nice room. And right next to the bus stop.
Mrs. Hunt:	Awfully noisy though, isn't it?
Estate Agent:	If you lived here, you'd hardly notice it. And it's so convenient for everything: buses, shops, doctor. Very important if your husband can't get about. If you put in double glazing you'd hardly notice the noise.
Mrs. Hunt:	What's that? Oh, someone playing the piano next door. Is that a partition wall?
Estate Agent:	Yes, that's right.
Mrs. Hunt:	Well, it's no good, if it's not fairly soundproof. My son plays the trombone, you see. We don't want to drive the neighbours mad.
Estate Agent:	Shall we take a look upstairs?
Mrs. Hunt:	Yes, all right. Lead the way. My word, these are steep stairs. I don't think my husband could manage these. We'd have to fit one of those invalid lifts up the stairway. I don't know ... it's an awful expense.

Recording Script

Estate Agent:	Perhaps he could have a bedroom downstairs, if you liked the house? There's plenty of room.
Mrs. Hunt:	The bathroom's up here though, isn't it?
Estate Agent:	This is a nice bedroom. Lovely long view from that window, right over the town.
Mrs. Hunt:	Yes, it's quite a nice room, and the decoration in here is quite pleasant, too. And what's next door? Oh, another bedroom. Dreadfully dark again.
Estate Agent:	Well these two rooms are directly over the two big rooms downstairs. This is the west-facing one. It gets all the afternoon sun.
Mrs. Hunt:	And across the landing?
Estate Agent:	That's the single bedroom. Here we are.
Mrs. Hunt:	Huh! It's tiny isn't it?
Estate Agent:	It's seven foot six, by five foot four. Plenty of room for a single bed.
Mrs. Hunt:	Well, fortunately my daughter only comes home in the holidays. But I do want some-where I can put visitors. There isn't anywhere to park, either, is there?
Estate Agent:	No, though you could knock down the front fence, and make a parking area in the front. People do.
Mrs. Hunt:	Well, we don't drive. But my daughter does. Oh ... I don't know.
Estate Agent:	And then there's the bathroom.
Mrs. Hunt:	Now, that is nice. I do like that. All the dark blue tiles, and the blue bath and everything. And he thick, white carpet. That does go with the house, doesn't it?
Estate Agent:	Yes, Mrs. Hunt. All the carpets and curtains are included.
Mrs. Hunt:	Because otherwise it's going to be out of our price range. We can only really afford $56,000 altogether. It's so expensive to move, these days.

Listening Two

Task b

Bellhop:	Well, here's your room, ma'am. Um ... after you.
Guest:	Well, thank you. Oh, what a nice, large room!
Bellhop:	Oh, yes, all the rooms here at the hotel are quite large, and the rooms on

	this side of the building have a lovely view. Let me open the drapes for you.
Guest:	Oh, you're right! The view is wonderful!
Bellhop:	Oh, yes, it is. Now, you'll find information about the facilities at the hotel in the directory, which is next to your telephone. (Mm-hmm.) Um, the TV is across the room in the corner, and you'll find your radio on the nightstand by the bed.
Guest:	Fine. I see. Thank you.
Bellhop:	Now, in the, uh, directory you'll find, uh, phone numbers and information about room service, our restaurants, and coffee shop. (Mm-hmm.) Uh, the two restaurants are on the second floor, and the coffee shop's in the lobby. (Right.) Oh, by the way, we have a lot of nice shops and boutiques here near the hotel, so you can do some shopping.
Guest:	Oh, that's wonderful. Thank you very much.
Bellhop:	Now, there's also a hairdresser and a newsstand just off the lobby to the right of the desk. I think the hairdresser is closed tomorrow on Monday. Uh, would you like me to check and see if the hair-dresser is open tomorrow?
Guest:	Uh ... no, no, no. That won't be necessary. Unless you really think I need it?
Bellhop:	Oh, no! No ma'am! Um ... now, you can call the housekeeper if you need your clothes pressed or your laundry done, and you can call the bell captain if you need something like a ... a taxi or an airport limo. Uh, we also have tickets to the theater a ... and, uh, sporting events. Of course, we can always help you with your luggage.
Guest:	Right. I see. Well, actually, there's only one thing I need to know. When is room service available?
Bellhop:	Oh, room service is available twenty-four hours a day here.
Guest:	Oh, good. Well, thank you very much.
Bellhop:	Yes. Now, we have a revolving cocktail lounge on the top floor and, uh, of course an Olympic-size pool and sauna in the basement. Um, the hours I think you'll find in the directory there. It's on the last page—
Guest:	I see. I see. Well, thank you so much. I ... I think I have it all down now. I'll be fine.
Bellhop:	Oh ... uh ... yes.
Guest:	Why don't you take this, uh ... just a little something for your trouble.
Bellhop:	Oh, thank you! Now, listen you have a pleasant stay.
Guest:	Thank you.

Recording Script

Unit 14 Stay Well

Listening One

Task b

Doctor: Oh, good morning, Mrs. Adams. What can I do for you?

Mrs. Adams: Hello, doctor, it's this ... I've got a pain in my back. It's ... it's really terrible during the day.

Doctor: Yes, does it ... does it hurt all the time?

Mrs. Adams: Well, after I've been doing the ... you know, bending, doing the housework and then when I ... if I stand up ... oh, it is so painful.

Doctor: Yes, yes, let me just feel there ... Is that where it is?

Mrs. Adams: Yes, that's it. Ooh!

Doctor: Yes, if I can just ... I think you've strained your back, obviously, rather badly. And I advise that you have plenty of rest. Don't do any heavy lifting. Don't do any lifting at all, actually. And ... um ... plenty of sleep. What sort of mattress do you sleep on?

Mrs. Adams: Well, we sleep on a soft mattress, of course ... er ...

Doctor: Yes, well, soft mattresses are not the best sort of mattress if you suffer from bad backs.

Mrs. Adams: Well, I've never had this before, you see, it's just recently come on me.

Doctor: Yes, well, if you could possibly get a harder mattress, it would be advisable.

Mrs. Adams: Yes, all right.

Doctor: All right, Mrs. Adams?

Mrs. Adams: Thank you very much, doctor.

Doctor: Thank you very much. Could you ask the next patient to come in, please?

Mr. Galway: Hello, doctor.

Doctor: Oh hello, Mr. Galway, how are you?

Mr. Galway: Well, you know, I hate to come bothering you really but ... er ... I was in ... walking in the street yesterday. Well, I was hurrying really, it's my own fault, and I tripped over and trying to save myself I ... I ... my wrist has ... has swollen up during the night something terrible.

Doctor:	Yes, I can see that. Oh, that's very nasty.
Mr. Galway:	I mean, I wouldn't have come up but the wife said, "Go ... go and see the doctor." Well I ...
Doctor:	You're very wise, Mr. Galway, could I just ...
Mr. Galway:	Oh!
Doctor:	... have a look? Oh, sorry. Does it hurt there?
Mr. Galway:	Well, it ... it ... just a bit, doctor, it ...
Doctor:	Yes, yes, yes, it's ...
Mr. Galway:	Oh dear! I think it's just a strain really.
Doctor:	Well, I'm not sure and because I'm not sure I'd like to send you to the hospital for an X-ray.
Mr. Galway:	Oh, I don't know about going to the hospital, doctor. Does it need all that much bother?
Doctor:	I think it would be wise, Mr. Galway, I really do. It would be advisable.
Mr. Galway:	All right, doctor, if you think so.
Doctor:	Yes, I think so.
Mr. Galway:	Do I make an appointment for myself?
Doctor:	I'll make the appointment for you Mr. Galway.
Mr. Galway:	Oh, no, I don't want to put you to no trouble, doctor.
Doctor:	That's quite all right, that's what I'm here for.
Mr. Galway:	Well, that's very nice of you.
Doctor:	Thank you very much.
Mr. Galway:	Thanks again, doctor. Hope I won't see you again, if you know what I mean!
Doctor:	Ha ha. Could you ask the next patient to come in please?
Mr. Galway:	I will ... I think you're next, gentleman there.
Mr. Finch:	Yes, thank you very much.
Doctor:	Oh hello, Mr. Finch and what can I do for you?
Mr. Finch:	Well it's ... er ... I've got this ... I've got this terrible cough.
Doctor:	You've still got the cough?
Mr. Finch:	Well, it doesn't seem to be getting any better.
Doctor:	Yes, well you know what I'm going to say, don't you, Mr. Finch?
Mr. Finch:	I know. I've tried. Look ... I ... I've tried and I've tried but I can't do it—I can't give them up.
Doctor:	Yes, I know ... Well, I'm afraid you have got to give them up, Mr.

Recording Script

	Finch. It's the only way you're going to get rid of that cough. Now, have you got any cigarettes on you at the moment?
Mr. Finch:	Er ... yeah, yeah.
Doctor:	I expect you have, yes. Could I just have a look at the packet? Yes? What I'm going to do with this packet is just throw them in the waste-paper basket, which is exactly what you're going to have to do. Mr. Finch, it's the only way.
Mr. Finch:	But I ... what ... can't you give me something else? I mean ...
Doctor:	There is nothing else, it's willpower, Mr. Finch.
Mr. Finch:	Oh well, I su ... I suppose you're right. I mean, I know you're right but I ... I don't seem to be able to do anything about it, that's the only thing.
Doctor:	Well, I think you must be determined ... and really work on that for a few weeks. Thank you.
Mr. Finch:	Sh ... shall I make an appointment to see you again?
Doctor:	Um ... make an appointment for a month's time, would you, Mr. Finch? And I do hope that you'll have given up smoking by then and the cough will have gone.
Mr. Finch:	Well, I shall ... er ... I'll try. Thank you.
Doctor:	Thank you Mr. Finch. Could you ask the next patient to come in, please?
Mr. Finch:	Yes, yes, fine.
Doctor:	Thank you.
Doctor:	Oh hello, Miss Talbot, what seems to be the trouble?
Miss Talbot:	Well, doctor, I'm having trouble sleeping.
Doctor:	Yes.
Miss Talbot:	I'm afraid I ... when I fall asleep ... er ... at night I tend to wake up very early in the morning and sometimes I don't sleep at all.
Doctor:	Oh dear, no, that's not very good, is it? Well, I would rather not prescribe sleeping tablets for you at the moment, I'd rather try other ways first. Um ... if before you go to bed you make a ... a nice hot drink and put some whisky in it. I think that would be a good idea.
Miss Talbot:	Oh ... er ... no, I'm sorry, no I ... I'm afraid I won't ... er ... I won't drink ... er ... no. Something hot and milky I have tried but it's ... er ... it doesn't work and ... um ...

Doctor:	I see ... I see. Well, in that case I will prescribe some very mild sleeping pills for you.
Miss Talbot:	Oh, that's wonderful, thank you.
Doctor:	And if you could come back and see me in, say, a fortnight and tell me how they work ...
Miss Talbot:	Indeed I will, thank you very much, doctor.
Doctor:	Thank you very much, Miss Talbot, goodbye.

Task c

1.

Ray:	Hey, Maria, how are you doing?
Maria:	Hi, Ray. All right, thanks. How are you?
Ray:	Maria, (Mm.) you look a little tired. (Oh.) Is everything okay?
Maria:	Well, yeah, I ... I am a little tired actually. I haven't been sleeping well. I only ... it takes me three or four hours to get to sleep each night.
Ray:	I bet you don't get enough exercise, huh?
Maria:	No, no, I think so. I walk to work every day. (Uh.) I play tennis twice a week.
Ray:	Oh. Well, that sounds pretty good. You know what you ought to do? (What's that?) You ought to do what I do. Drink a little hot milk ...
Maria:	Oh, everybody tells (Uh.) me to drink hot milk. (No, no, no, no.) But I hate hot milk.
Ray:	No. Let me finish. You drink a little hot milk (Uh-huh.) with a little brandy in it before going to bed.
Maria:	Oh, brandy. Oh. Well, that ... that sounds much better. I'll try that tonight. Thank you.
Ray:	Hey, Maria.
Maria:	Yeah?
Ray:	Let me know how it works out, okay?

2.

Don:	Oh, my—ugh!
Beth:	Don, what's wrong?
Don:	Oh, I am in such pain. My back's been hurting me for like the last two days.
Beth:	Oh, I know how that is. I have back pains myself.
Don:	Oh, you do?
Beth:	Say, do you have a heating pad?
Don:	No.

Recording Script

Beth:	I could lend you one. It really helps.
Don:	Oh, anything. Thank you.
Beth:	Sure. Do you have a hard mattress?
Don:	No, no. I like a nice soft mattress.
Beth:	Oh, that's it. You should put a board under the mattress to make it firmer.
Don:	Why?
Beth:	Well, because—don't you know? Soft mattresses are bad for the back.
Don:	Oh, the back!
Beth:	You know, I've got some exercises that my doctor told me about.
Don:	Yeah?
Beth:	Yeah. Ah ... this one really worked for me.
Don:	What?
Beth:	See, you lie down on the floor with your knees on your chest.
Don:	Uh-huh.

3.

Woman:	Well, the salad's almost ready. How's the chili doing? I'm starving.
Man:	So am I. The chili looks just about ready. One final taste and-ow!
Woman:	Oooo, oooo, what's the matter? Oooo.
Man:	Oh, my finger, I burned my finger!
Woman:	Oh, wait, I'll get an ice cube and put on it.
Man:	Okay, okay.
Woman:	There.
Man:	Ah, ah, much better.
Woman:	How's it feel?
Man:	Oh, it feels good.
Woman:	Good.
Man:	Feels good. Ah, thanks. Let's eat.
Woman:	Okay.

4.

Jennifer:	My throat is really sore.
Patrick:	Have you tried putting a spoonful of honey and some hot water with lemon juice?
Jennifer:	You know, I never did like honey. Ugh.
Patrick:	No? Well, why don't you try some tea, some hot tea?
Jennifer:	Oh, Patrick, I don't know.

Patrick: Well, I don't know either. I mean, maybe you could stop smoking so many cigarettes.

Jennifer: Patrick, get off my back. I'll take care of it.

Listening Two

Task b

1.

A: Hello.

B: Hi, It's Marty. How are you? We missed you at the game today.

A: Yeah. I've been in bed for a couple of days.

B: Oh gee. What's wrong?

A: Oh, I'm just a little under the weather, I guess. My nose is stopped up and I've just felt crummy.

B: Yeah, everybody seems to have something that's going around. Have you seen a doctor?

A: No. I just got some non-prescription nasal spray at the drugstore and I'm drinking plenty of fluids. One more day of rest and I'm sure I'll be back to work. I had chills the first day and my stomach was upset, but now it's really only my nose.

B: Well that's good. Listen, I won't keep you any longer. I'm sure you'll want to rest. Do you think you'll be going to the game on Wednesday?

A: Oh, I'm sure I'll be fine by then.

B: Great. Well, take care. I'll see you on Wednesday.

A: Yeah. Thanks for calling.

B: Bye.

2.

A: OK, Mike. You said it's around your stomach. Please take off your shirt.

B: OK ... This rash is all over my right leg, too, Doctor.

A: I'll just look at that in just a minute. Have you been out in the woods lately?

B: Yes, I went for a hike in the country on Saturday.

A: Uh-huh; and when did you first notice the rash?

B: On Monday. At first I thought it was just a little skin irritation, but then it started to swell up, and I was very uncomfortable. I washed it with antiseptic soap, but that didn't seem to help, and by Thursday, it started to itch and burn.

A: Did you notice you had a fever or not?

Recording Script

B: I didn't take my temperature, but aside from the itching, I feel fine.
A: And, any difficulty breathing?
B: No.
A: Sore throat or runny nose?
B: No.
A: OK. I think you're going to be fine. I'm going to prescribe some cream that will help with the rash.
B: Thanks, doctor.
A: And make sure to thoroughly wash all clothing that you were wearing during your hike last Saturday.

3.

A: What is it, Lou? Your stomach again?
B: No, no ... I'm all right.
A: Lou, I can tell when you get that look on your face.
B: It's nothing. Probably too much food at dinner. Ooh ... Uh!
A: Lou, that's it! You're going back to the doctor tomorrow. This has gone on too long!
B: No ... Listen, I'll take some Fizz-Away and I'll be fine in the morning.
A: Fizz-Away? Fizz-Away is an over-the-counter antacid. That's not going to help you, Lou. Your problem is too serious for antacid to help you. You know, if you don't watch out, you're going to end up on the surgeon's table just like your brother.
B: Oh, don't be silly. He never took care of himself and drank like a fish. It's different with me. I just eat a little too much sometimes.
A: Look, this is a problem that runs in your family. Your father had it, your brother, your uncle Leo ...
B: Mindy, this is not a hereditary condition.
A: No, but they say lifestyle and poor eating habits create the problem and that is something that you get from your family.
B: Listen, this is ridiculous. Ooh ... Ow ... Oh! Where's the Fizz-Away? It's burning.
A: Oh, Lou. This can't go on.
B: Look, it was probably the fried chicken at dinner.
A: Here, take this. Now I'm not taking no for an answer. You're going to the doctor tomorrow and that's final. Fried chicken! How come I don't have any pain? I ate the same food that you had.
B: Oh, okay, okay; I'll go. Ow!

Task d

Dr. Martin Answay writes a column in a popular women's magazine on health problems. He is also an expert on heart disease.

Q: Dr. Answay. Is there a secret to good health? I mean, is there some way we can achieve it which is not generally known?

A: It certainly isn't a secret. However, there is a great deal of ignorance, even among supposedly educated people, about how to be reasonably healthy.

Q: Well, what advice do you give, then?

A: Uh ... to begin with, take diet. I believe that one of the greatest dangers to health in Britain and other countries ... particularly developed countries ... is the kind of food we tend to prefer.

Q: Such as?

A: Such as that great national institution, the British breakfast, for example. Ham and eggs. Or the kind of lunch so many people in this country have: sausage and chips! Or all the convenience foods like hamburgers. Or even things we regard as "healthy", such as full-fat milk. Or Cheddar cheese. The list is endless.

Q: What's wrong with those things?

A: The excessive consumption of such things leads to the overproduction of cholesterol, which in turn results in heart atta ...

Q: Excuse me, but what exactly is cholesterol?

A: It's a ... wax-like substance ... yellowish ... and it's produced naturally in our livers. We all need some cholesterol for survival.

Q: Well, if we need it, in what way is it bad for us?

A: Too much of it is bad for us. It builds up in our arteries, causing them to get narrower, so that our blood has difficulty in getting through ... and this, of course, can eventually end in a heart attack or stroke. The point I'm trying to make here is that, even though we all need some cholesterol in order to insulate our nerves, and to produce cell membranes and hormones, the things many of us eat and even consider healthy lead to the overproduction of cholesterol. And this is very dangerous.

Q: So, how can we avoid this overproduction of cholesterol?

A: By cutting down our consumption of animal fats: things like red meat, cheese, eggs, and so on. And by increasing our consumption of fresh fruit and vegetables, and also by eating more potatoes, rice, pasta and bread.

Q: Pasta? Potatoes? But ... aren't such things fattening?

A: Nonsense. It isn't pasta, potatoes or bread that makes us fat. It's what we put on such things! Cheese. Butter. Meat!

Q: So anything we like, anything that's delicious, is bad for us. Isn't that what you're saying?

A: Rubbish! I'm simply saying we eat too much of these things. And there are many ways of preparing delicious food without using such large quantities of animal fats.

Q: Last of all, what about exercise? You recently warned against certain forms of exercise, which you said could be dangerous.

A: What I said was that if people aren't used to getting regular and vigorous exercise, they should begin slowly, and not try to do too much at the beginning! I also said that certain games, such as squash, can be dangerous, particularly if you aren't used to playing them. A number of injuries are due to the sudden, twisting movements that games like squash involve.

Q: So, what kinds of exercise do you recommend, then?

A: Gentle jogging, swimming, cycling, brisk walking ... exercise that is rhythmic and gentle, and above all, sustained. That is, done for at least fifteen minutes uninterruptedly at least three times a week. We all need such exercise, and the fact is that far too few of us get enough of it, particularly if we live in large cities and regularly use cars.

Unit 15   What's My Line?

Listening One

Task b

Catherine has just left school and she wants to find a job. She and her mother have come to speak to the Careers Advisory Officer. Listen to their conversation.

Officer: Oh, come in, take a seat. I'm the Careers Officer. You're Cathy, aren't you?

Mother: That's right. This is Catherine Hunt, and I'm her mother.

Officer: How do you do, Mrs. Hunt. Hello, Catherine.

Cathy: Hello. Pleased to meet you.

Officer: And you'd like some advice about choosing a career?

Mother: Yes, she would. Wouldn't you, Catherine?

Cathy: Yes, please.

Officer: Well, just let me ask a few questions to begin with. How old are you, Catherine?

Mother: She's nineteen. Well, she's almost nineteen. She'll be nineteen next month.

Officer: And what qualifications have you got?

Mother: Well, qualifications from school of course. Very good results she got. And she's got certificates for ballet and for playing the piano.

Officer: Is that what you're interested in, Catherine, dancing and music?

Cathy: Well ...

Mother: Ever since she was a little girl she's been very keen on her music and dancing. She ought to be a music teacher or something. She's quite willing to train for a few more years to get the right job, aren't you, Catherine?

Cathy: Well, if it's a good idea.

Mother: There you are, you see. She's a good girl really. A bit lazy and disorganised sometimes, but she's very bright. I'm sure the Careers Officer will have lots of jobs for you.

Officer: Well, I'm afraid it's not as easy as that. There are many young people these days who can't find the job they want.

Mother: I told you so, Catherine. I told you that you shouldn't wear that dress. You have to look smart to get a job these days.

Officer: I think she looks very nice. Mrs. Hunt, will you come into the other office for a moment and look at some of the information we have there. I'm sure you'd like to see how we can help young people.

Mother: Yes, I'd love to. Mind you, I think Catherine would be a very nice teacher. She could work with young children. She'd like that. Or she could be a vet. She's always looking after sick animals.

Officer: I'm afraid there's a lot of competition. You need very good results to be a vet. This way, Mrs. Hunt. Just wait a minute, Catherine.

Officer: There are just one or two more things, Catherine.

Cathy: Do call me Cathy.

Officer: OK, Cathy. Are you really interested in being a vet?

Cathy: Not really. Anyway, I'm not bright enough. I'm reasonably intelligent, but I'm not brilliant. I'm afraid my mother is a bit over-optimistic.

Officer: Yes, I guessed that. She's a bit overpowering, isn't she, your mum?

Cathy: A bit. But she's very kind.

Officer: I'm sure she is. So, you're interested in ballet and music, are you?

Recording Script

Cathy:	Not really. My mother sent me to lessons when I was six, so I'm quite good, I suppose. But I don't want to do that for the rest of my life, especially music. It's so lonely.
Officer:	What do you enjoy doing?
Cathy:	Well, I like playing tennis, and swimming. Oh, I went to France with the school choir last year. I really enjoyed that. And I like talking to people. But I suppose you mean real interests—things that would help me to get a job?
Officer:	No. I'm more interested in what you really want to do. You like talking to people, do you?
Cathy:	Oh yes, I really enjoy meeting new people.
Officer:	Do you think you would enjoy teaching?
Cathy:	No, no, I don't really. I was never very interested in school work, and I'd like to do something different. Anyway, there's a teacher training college very near us. It would be just like going to school again.
Officer:	So you don't want to go on training?
Cathy:	Oh, I wouldn't mind at all, not for something useful. I wondered about being a hairdresser—you meet lots of people, and you learn to do something properly—but I don't know. It doesn't seem very worthwhile.
Officer:	What about nursing?
Cathy:	Nursing? In a hospital? Oh, I couldn't do that, I'm not good enough.
Officer:	Yes, you are. You've got good qualifications in English and Maths. But it is very hard work.
Cathy:	Oh, I don't mind that.
Officer:	And it's not very pleasant sometimes.
Cathy:	That doesn't worry me either. Mum's right. I do look after sick animals. I looked after our dog when it was run over by a car. My mother was sick, but I didn't mind. I was too worried about the dog. Do you really think I could be a nurse?
Officer:	I think you could be a very good nurse. You'd have to leave home, of course.
Cathy:	I rather think I should enjoy that.
Officer:	Well, don't decide all at once. Here's some information about one or two other things which might suit you. Have a look through it before you make up your mind.

Task d

Interview 1

Applicant: A bit of cinema, a bit of reading. You know ... I don't really have very much free time, really. In my current job I quite often have to work on Saturdays and Sundays, or late at night when the computers can be turned off—we sometimes can't do much during the day because everyone's using their machines.

Interviewer: OK, great. Perhaps we can turn to this job now. First of all, why do you want to work for us?

Applicant: I think because yours is the biggest company in the field. I'm really interested in modern communications, and the biggest company should offer the biggest opportunities.

Interviewer: And what are your strengths and weaknesses?

Applicant: Weaknesses? I haven's got any! And strengths? Ambition, I really want to do well, and I'm flexible and reliable.

Interviewer: Why do you think you'd be good at this job?

Applicant: Oh, um, why would I be good? I don't know really ... I just think I'd be good at it; I mean, I know a lot about systems support, and this seems to be the perfect job for me.

Interviewer: Where do you want to be in five years' time?

Applicant: I want to progress within the organization. I'd like more responsibility, and more money too, if possible!

Interviewer: Speaking of money, could I ask you a few details about your current salary and extras?

Applicant: Yes, sure. Well, I'm earning 19,000 at the moment, but then I get some overtime on top of that, so I suppose altogether it comes to more like twenty-two. And I'm a member of the company pension scheme which is good for the future.

Interview 2

Applicant: Yeah, the traffic was terrible, and the weather. It took me ages to get here, and then I couldn't find the car park! I'll just put my umbrella in the corner here, shall I? Anyway, I'm really sorry I'm late.

Interviewer: Well, I'm glad you got here in the end. Now, we should probably get going as fast as we can, because I've got another interview at 12:00. I think the most important question I can ask is "Why do you want to

Recording Script

	work for us?"
Applicant:	Well, I'm a bit bored where I'm working at the moment, so I'd really like a change. I mean, I've been there for nearly a year now. I don't know if I'll like it more here, but it's a bigger company, and the salary's a lot better than the job I've got. Also, I like the idea of flexitime, because I find it really hard to get up in the morning!
Interviewer:	And what would you say your main strengths and weaknesses are?
Applicant:	Strengths? A sense of humour. And weaknesses? Well, everybody says I'm really disorganized, but I don't think I am. I'm sometimes a bit late, you know, for meetings and deadlines, but I usually survive! I think I'm reliable. I always do what I say I'm going to do, eventually.
Interviewer:	Why do you think you'd be good at this job?
Applicant:	Oh … hmm, that's a difficult question, Well, I've got the right qualifications. I'm interested, and like a challenge. I'm quite independent, too.
Interviewer:	And where do you want to be in five years' time?
Applicant:	Australia, I hope! I mean I'm planning to stay in Britain for a year or two, but to be honest I really want to move somewhere hot and sunny. And after a couple of years I'll probably feel like another change.
Interviewer:	Ok, And what about your free time? What sort of things do you do?
Applicant:	Um, well, I like to keep my weekends completely free—I hate having, having to work at the weekend, because I go walking. I try to get up to Scotland whenever I can. And I play a lot of sport, tennis, squash, things like that, you know …

Listening Two

Task a

First speaker: I'm a night person. I love the hours, you know? I like going to work at around six at night and then getting home at two or three in the morning. I like being out around people, you know, talking to them, listening to their problems. Some of my regulars are always on the lookout for ways that they can stump me. Like last week, one of them came in and asked for a Ramos gin fizz. He didn't think I knew how to make it. Hah! But I know how to make every drink in the book, and then some. Although some of the nights when I go in I just don't feel like dealing with all the noise. When I get in a big crowd it can be pretty noisy. People talking, the sound system blaring, the pinball machine, the video games. And then at the end of the night you don't always smell so good, either. You smell like cigarettes. But I like the place and I plan on sticking around for a while.

Second speaker: If I had to sit behind a desk all day, I'd go crazy! I'm really glad I have a job where I can keep moving, you know? My favorite part is picking out the music—I use new music for every ten-week session. For my last class I always use the Beatles-it's a great beat to move to, and everybody loves them. I like to sort of educate people about their bodies, and show them you know, how to do the exercises and movements safely. Like, it just kills me when I see people trying to do sit-ups with straight legs—it's so bad for your back! And ... let's see ... I—I like to see people make progress—at the end of a session you can really see how people have slimmed down and sort of built up some muscle—it's very gratifying.

The part I don't like is, well, it's hard to keep coming up with new ideas for classes. I mean, you know, there are just so many ways you can move your body, and it's hard to keep coming up with interesting routines and ... and new exercises. And it's hard on my voice—I have to yell all the time so people can hear me above the music, and like after three classes in one day my voice has had it. Then again, having three classes in one day has its compensations—I can eat just about anything I want and not gain any weight.

Third speaker: What do I like about my job? Money. M-O-N-E-Y. No, I like the creativity, and I like my studio. All my tools are like toys to me—you know, my watercolors, pens and inks, colored pencils, drafting table—I love playing with them. And I have lots of different kinds of clients—I do magazines, book covers, album covers, newspaper articles—so there's lots of variety, which I like. You know, sometimes when I start working on a project I could be doing it for hours and have no conception of how much time has gone by—what some people call a flow experience. I don't like the pressure, though, and there's plenty of it in this business, You're always working against a tight deadline. And I don't like the business end of it—you know, contacting clients for work, negotiating contracts, which get long and complicated.

Fourth speaker: Well, I'll tell you. At first it was fun, because there was so much to learn, and working with figures and money was interesting. But after about two years the thrill was gone, and now it's very routine. I keep the books, do the payroll, pay the taxes, pay the insurance, pay the bills. I hate paying the bills, because there's never enough money to pay them! I also don't like the pressure of having to remember when all the bills and taxes are due. And my job requires a lot of reading that I don't particularly enjoy—like, I have to keep up to date on all the latest tax forms, and it's pretty dull. I like it when we're making money, though, because I get to see all my efforts rewarded.

Recording Script

Task b

Martin Johnson is the manager of an employment agency. People who want a job come to his office, and Martin writes some information about each person on a card. Then he puts the information into the computer. When someone telephones the office and asks for a person to do a job, Martin programs the computer to find the right person for the job. But this morning it is different. Martin picks up the telephone, and this is the conversation …

Martin:	Good morning, Johnson Employment Agency. Can I help you?
Mr. Saunders:	I hope so. My name is Patrick Saunders. I'm a photographer. I rang you yesterday.
Martin:	Oh yes, Mr. Saunders, I remember. I spoke to you myself. You wanted a young lady to help you with some advertisements, didn't you?
Mr. Saunders:	That's right. Do you remember what I said?
Martin:	More or less, I think. You said you wanted a young lady with red hair and green eyes, I remember. You said you had to model an evening dress.
Mr. Saunders:	That's right.
Martin:	And you said she had to be tall. Over six feet, I think you said.
Mr. Saunders:	That's right.
Martin:	And slim. You said you were looking for someone tall and slim with red hair. You gave me the measurements.
Mr. Saunders:	That's right.
Martin:	Yes, I remember. It was very difficult to find anyone. Not many women are six feet tall, and not many tall young women have red hair and green eyes. But we found someone in the end. I telephoned you last night and said that we were sending someone this morning.
Mr. Saunders:	Yes, that's right.
Martin:	She wasn't late, was she? You said the studio opened at nine, and you wanted the young lady at half past.
Mr. Saunders:	That's right. I needed to buy some more film. I opened the studio and went into town. I left a note for the person that you sent. I said I wouldn't be long, and that I wanted to start work as soon as I came back. I said that the evening dress was in the cupboard.
Martin:	Yes, I see …
Mr. Saunders:	I left instructions to go behind the screen and put on the evening

205

	dress. I left a necklace and a bracelet with the evening dress. I asked the person to put them on carefully, because they were valuable.
Martin:	And what happened? Didn't anyone come?
Mr. Saunders:	Oh, yes, someone came.
Martin:	You haven't lost the jewellery?
Mr. Saunders:	Oh no, everything is still here. Who did you send?
Martin:	Let me look at my book. Yes, here it is. We sent someone called J.V. Brown. Why? Did someone else arrive?
Mr. Saunders:	No, no. J.V. Brown came to the studio at half-past nine, found the note and put on the evening dress and the jewellery.
Martin:	Isn't that what you said you wanted?
Mr. Saunders:	Not exactly.
Martin:	What do you mean ... not exactly?
Mr. Saunders:	J.V. Brown is standing in the studio now. He is a shortish, fat man, with a bald head and a beard. He is forty-five years old and has got broad shoulders and hairy arms. At the moment he is wearing a green satin dress. He looks very odd.
Martin:	There must be some mistake!
Mr. Saunders:	Yes, I think so. He told me he was a plumber.
Martin:	Did we send him?
Mr. Saunders:	Yes, you did. He said he was very surprised when he got your message, but he was pleased to find a job. The note said that he was going to be in advertisements. It asked him to be here at half-past nine.
Martin:	This is astonishing. I don't know how it happened.
Mr. Saunders:	He came and found my message, so he put on the dress and waited. When I came he told me that he felt very silly, but he thought it was the costume for the advertisement. The dress is much too tight, and much too long. He's wearing the necklace but not the bracelet. He told me his arm was too big.
Martin:	Well, the computer can't be wrong ... wait a minute, I'll look on my address cards. Oh dear, I know what's happened!
Mr. Saunders:	What?
Martin:	We've got two people called J.V. Brown. We've sent you the wrong one. I'm terribly sorry.
Mr. Saunders:	Oh. Well, I'll send J.V. Brown back to you. I'm going to take some photographs anyway. A short, fat, baldheaded man in an evening

	dress is certainly unusual.
Martin:	The trouble is, that's not all. Somewhere in London a tall, red-headed beauty queen is trying to mend the drains!

Unit 16 Making Your Point

Listening One

Task b

Presenter:	Thank you all for attending this panel discussion on the long term effects of corporal punishment—specifically spanking or hitting children as a form of discipline. Before we open the discussion up to questions from our audience, I would like to give our expert speakers a chance to summarize their points. The first is Donald Sterling, a lawyer and psychologist who interviews criminals before they go to trial.
Sterling:	I've seen it over and over again. Violent criminals were almost always spanked and hit when they were children. This corporal punishment teaches children to be violent when they are very young, so when they are adults, they commit crimes and abuse their wives and children. And then their children grow up to be violent, and the cycle continues.
Presenter:	Next is Dr. Phyllis Jones from Center for Family Research.
Jones:	We studied 332 families to see how parents' actions affected teenagers' behavior. We found that teenagers did better when they had clear discipline as a child. Some of these parents used spanking as a form of discipline, and some didn't. It seems that spanking doesn't hurt children if it's done in a loving home, but it's most important to talk to your children and spend time with them. Spanking should be the choice of the parents.
Presenter:	And finally, Lois Goldin, a child psychologist.
Goldin:	In the United States, the number of parents who spank their kids is decreasing, and people who oppose spanking say that's good because it will make our society less violent. But look at statistics. Actually, violent crime is rising every year and the number of teenagers and children that commit crimes is going up the fastest! Parents need to control their children better, and corporal punishment is one way to do that.

Presenter: My thanks to our three speakers. Now our guests will be happy to answer questions from the audience.

Task c

Teacher: Good morning. Did anyone hear the news about the teenager in New York who hacked into a bank's database and stole about 30,000 credit card numbers over the weekend? Hacking is related to computer ethics—that's our topic today.

Computer ethics deals with the proper use of information technology, such as computers and the Internet. By proper use, I mean socially responsible use. We'll first talk about what ethical behavior is, and how this applies to computer use.

First, I want to make sure we all know what ethic is. Anyone? Yes, John.

Student 1: It's about right and wrong.

Teacher: Yes. OK, Jennifer.

Student 2: And it's about being a good person, doing what's right.

Teacher: Yes, ethics includes both of these ideas. It deals with moral judgments, with what is acceptable or unacceptable to do. Now we learn ideas about what is right and wrong from our families, our friends, and from the culture we live in. Because of differences in our backgrounds, we may not always agree on what is right and wrong.

However, for our discussion today, I will define for you what I mean by an ethical action. An ethical action is something someone does that benefits someone and doesn't hurt anyone. So, for example, if you see a man drop some money, and you pick the money up and give it to him. This is an ethical action. On the other hand, if you pick up the money and don't give it back to the man. This benefits you, but hurts the man. This is not an ethical action.

Now what about computers? What are the ethical boundaries for using computers and the Internet? Most people agree that it is wrong to steal from a store. Would they also say it is wrong to copy music files from the Internet? Or, to take another example, most people agree that it is wrong to open and envelope and read a letter to someone else. Would they also say it's wrong to read someone else's e-mail?

In the past decade or so, many more people have started using computers and the Internet, so these issues have become important. In 1992, the Computer Ethics Institute was founded in the United States. This is a research, education, and policy study group whose goal is to increase awareness of the ethical issues that are likely to come up as technology develops.

One concept the Computer Ethics Institute has developed is the Ten Commandments of Computer Ethics. These rules are important guidelines the Institute thinks all computer users should follow. Now some of you may be familiar with the Ten Commandments from the Bible, like, uh, "Thou shalt not kill." or "Thou shalt honor thy father and thy mother." The Ten Commandments of Computer Ethics have been written in the same style of language used in the Ten Commandments from the Bible. For example, they use the phrase "Thou shalt not ..." "Thou shalt not ..." means "don't" or "you shouldn't" .

Let's look at each commandment or rule.

The first commandment says: Thou shalt not use a computer to harm other people. Simple enough, right?

Number Two. Thou shalt not interfere with other people's computer work. I interpret this to mean don't use a computer in any way that will affect or change the work someone else is doing. Don't move or edit someone else's files without telling them.

Number Three. Thou shalt not snoop in other people's files. To snoop means to try to find out something without another person knowing it. If you look at someone else's files on the computer or read their e-mail, you're snooping. Respect other people's privacy.

Number Four. Thou shalt not use a computer to steal. There are situations on the Internet in which you have to decide if you are stealing or not, like downloading music files, as I mentioned earlier.

Number Five. Thou shalt not use a computer to say things that are untrue. It is up to you to be truthful in your website, in your e-business, and in your e-mail.

Number Six. Thou shalt not use software for which you have not paid. In other words, if the software is free on the Internet, it's Okay to download and use it. However, it is not okay to copy software from a friend, because you didn't pay for it.

Number Seven. Thou shalt not use other people's computer resources without telling them, or without paying them. For example, you shouldn't use someone else's computer, password, or Internet connection without asking them first.

Number Eight. Thou shalt not appropriate someone else's ideas. Appropriate is spelled A-P-P-R-O-P-R-I-A-T-E. It means to take words someone else wrote and say they're yours. Uh, for example, you have to write a report for school. If you copy a term paper from the Internet and hand it in, you're breaking the rule. Copying even a few sentences off the Internet and presenting them as your own is breaking the rule.

Number Nine. The ninth commandment says: Thou shalt think about the social consequences of the program you are writing. Now this applies mostly to computer programrs. Social consequences means how the program you're writing might affect others in society. Could hackers possibly use your own program to illegally gain access to a computer system? Skillful hackers can hack into banks and into credit card companies; they can alter accounts and steal money. They can also create viruses that can cause billions of dollars of damage worldwide.

Number Ten. The tenth commandment says: Thou shalt always use a computer in ways that are respectful of others. For example, sending unfriendly e-mail to someone or about someone or creating websites with negative messages are examples of breaking this rule.

OK, the Computer Ethics Institute has sent these guidelines to many large companies and to schools across the United States. However, there's no way to enforce these rules. Nevertheless, they would like to see schools, in particular, utilize these rules to help students develop a strong sense of computer ethics. OK, any questions or comments at this point?

Listening Two

Task a

1.

Clerk:	Hello, sir. What can I do for you?
Customer:	Hi. Uh ... I have this ... uh ... cassette player (Mm-hmm.) here that I bought about six months ago. And it just ruined four of my favorite cassettes.
Clerk:	Oh dear, I'm sorry.
Customer:	So, I ... um ... wanted you to fix it. I'm sure it will be no problem, right?
Clerk:	Your sales slip, please?
Customer:	Yeah, here it is. Uh.
Clerk:	I'm sorry, sir. Your warranty's expired.
Customer:	Well, it ... uh ... ran out ten days ago, but I'm sure that you'll ... you'll ... fix the machine for free, because the machine was obviously defective when I bought it. I ...
Clerk:	I'm sorry. sir. Your warranty has run out. There's nothing I can do.

Recording Script

Customer: No. No, look. No. I didn't drop it off a building or anything. I mean, what difference can ten days make? I mean you ... you can—
Clerk: Sir, I'm sorry, we have the six-month rule for a reason. We can't ...
Customer: Well, but you can bend the rule a little bit.
Clerk: ... make an exception for you. Then we'll have to make an exception for everybody. (Well, but look ...) You could say its only a month, it's only two months.
Customer: I just lost twenty dollars worth of tapes.
Clerk: Sir, I'm sorry, it's too late.
Customer: It actually ate the tapes. I mean, they're destroyed. I mean-
Clerk: Well, sir, you knew (I ...) when your warranty ran out. You should (Well ...) have brought it in before. It was (Well ... look ...) guaranteed for six months. I'm sorry, there's nothing I can do.
Customer: Paying for this is adding insult to injury. I mean, surely you're going to make good on this cassette player. It's ... it's ... it's a good cassette player, but it's just defective. I mean, I can't pay for this.
Clerk: Well, sir, I'm sorry, you should have brought it in earlier.
Customer: But surely you won't hold me to ten days on this.
Clerk: Sir, the rules are the rules. I'm sorry, but there's nothing I can do.

2.
Norma: You know, Brian, it doesn't look like you've vacuumed the living room or cleaned the bathroom.
Brian: No, I haven't. Ugh. I had the worst day. I am so tired. Look, I promise I'll do it this weekend.
Norma: Listen, I know the feeling. I'm tired, too. But I came home and I did my share of the housework. I mean, that's the agreement, right?
Brian: All right. We agreed. I'll do it in a minute.
Norma: Come on. Don't be that way. You know, I shouldn't have to ask you to do anything. I mean, we both work, we both live in the house, we agreed that housework is ... is both of our responsibility. I don't like to have to keep reminding you about it. It makes me feel like an old nag or something.
Brian: Sometimes you are an old nag.
Norma: Oh, great!
Brian: No, it's just that I don't notice when things get dirty like you do. Look,

	all you have to do is tell me, and I'll do it.
Norma:	No, I don't want to be put in that position. I mean, you can see dirt as well as I can. Otherwise—I mean, that puts all the responsibility on me.
Brian:	it's just that cleanliness is not a high priority with me. There are other things I would much rather do. Besides, the living room floor does not look that dirty.
Norma:	Brian.
Brian:	Okay, a couple crumbs.

3.

Bob:	Mr. Weaver, I have been with this company now for five years. And I've always been very loyal to the company. And I feel that I've worked quite hard here. And I've never been promoted. It's getting to the point now in my life where, you know, I need more money. I would like to buy a car. I'd like to start a family, and maybe buy a house, all of which is impossible with the current salary you're paying me.
Mr. Weaver:	Bob, I know you've been with the company for a while, but raises here are based on merit, not on length of employment. Now, you do your job adequately, but you don't do it well enough to deserve a raise at this time. Now, I've told you before, to earn a raise you need to take more initiative and show more enthusiasm for the job. Uh, for instance, maybe find a way to make the office run more efficiently.
Bob:	All right. Maybe I could show a little more enthusiasm. I still think that, I work hard here. But a company does have at least an obligation to pay its employees enough to live on. And the salary I'm getting here isn't enough. I mean, rents are rising. The price of food is going up. Inflation is high. And I can barely cover my expenses.
Mr. Weaver:	Bob, again, I pay people what they're worth to the company, now, not what they think they need to live on comfortably. If you did that, the company would go out of business.
Bob:	Yes, but I have ... I have been here for five years and I have been very loyal. And it's absolutely necessary for me to have a raise or I cannot justify keeping this job any more.
Mr. Weaver:	Well, that's a decision you'll have to make for yourself, Bob.

Recording Script

Task b

Woman A: Did you hear on the news today about that ... uh ... murderer who was executed?

Woman B: I can't believe it.

Woman A: Yeah. That's the first time in ten years that they've used capital punishment.

Woman B: I just can't believe in our society today that they would actually kill another human being. Nobody has the right to take another person's life.

Woman A: Oh, I don't agree. Listen, I think capital punishment is—it's about time it came back. I think that's exactly what killers deserve.

Woman B: No, they don't deserve that. Because once you're killing a killer, you're the killer, too. You become a killer as well.

Woman A: No, listen. You take a life, you have to be willing to give up your own. And also, I think that if you have a death penalty it will prevent other people from killing. I think it's a good deterrent.

Woman B: I don't think it's a deterrent at all. My goodness gracious. I mean, first of all, are you sure the person you've convicted to death is really guilty?

Woman A: Well, I think that's a very rare ... very rare incidence.

Woman B: I don't think it's rare, (I don't think it's ...) with all the crackerjack lawyers we have today, (Well, no ... I ...) and the judicial system the way it is.

Woman A: I think it's a rare incidence, and I think it's more important to get rid of the ... the bad seed, you know?

Woman B: But you don't get rid of it. You rehabilitate somebody like that. (Oh ...) You don't eliminate, you rehabilitate.

Woman A: Listen, studies show that criminals are never really rehabilitated. When they're ... when they come out of prison they just go back to a life of crime, and they're hardened by that crime.

Woman B: Because the rehabilitation process has to be more than just what's in the jail. I mean, (Oh ... well.) when you're in jail you do have to work, but when you're out of jail there has to be an extensive program. We have to expand on the idea till it works.

Woman A: I don't agree. Listen—and, anyway, the jails and the prisons are already very crowded, and we have to pay, the taxpayers. Our money goes to maintaining murderers' (I ...) lives.

Woman B: I agree with you. That's why it's important to look at the problem on a much larger scale. The real problem is a social problem. (What ... no ...) There are other problems that cause people to kill. Look at poverty, drugs, discrimination.

Woman A: Some people are just bad. They're just evil and there's nothing you can do.

Woman B: No, there ... it is ... no, it isn't true. There's rehabilitation. (No.) And they ... we're all responsible it ... for ... to humanity. That's one of the reasons ...

Woman A: Well, but in the meantime you have to take care of the people who have already committed ...

Woman B: I agree with you there.

Woman A: Preventative is different, but ...

Woman B: I agree with you there.

Unit 17 Sports

Listening One

Task b

1. Alison

Alison: I took up swimming not only to get exercise but to rid myself of stresses, and to go swimming at the end of the day when I'd been in the office all day was a very good way of shaking off the office before you go home for the evening or go out with friends.

2. Susanna

Susanna: That's right, it was a kind of mixture of aerobics, a bit of yoga and what they call stretch exercises, which is kind of ... erm, well you kind of stretch into a position and hold it, which is supposed to be very good for you. And it was all done to music—it was very jolly, it was a very jolly teacher, who's very careful you didn't do too much and, erm, there were young, mostly young women there, as you'd expect, but there was a big, fat old man called George who also ... who did quite well, and his girlfriend, Mavis or whatever, and it was quite fun.

Recording Script

3. Tim

Tim: Basically, because I'm overweight and I feel I've got this flabby belt around my stomach and, er, the only way of really getting rid of it is through weight-training.

4. Iain

John: Er, what kind of exercise do you take?

Iain: Erm, I take part in, erm, amateur athletics, erm, er, three or four times a week. Er, predominantly track running, as opposed to cross country or road racing.

John: And why do you do that? Is it for pleasure, or to, erm, keep fit, or ...?

Iain: It's a combination of those. Erm, I have a fairly sedentary job, therefore I like to have some exercise to compensate that. Erm, but I also believe in keeping reasonably fit, erm, in myself, anyway.

5. Bridget

Bridget: I prefer yuga.

Brenda: Ah.

Bridget: Mmm.

Brenda: Why do you like that ... like yoga?

Bridget: Um, because I feel that it ... well, one of the principles is that you don't push the body further than it can go, so that I think the self-punishing aspect isn't there. Erm, and I always feel, erm, very well in myself afterwards; whereas after aerobics I may feel quite, erm, revived, because exercise does generate energy, but I don't ... I still feel that I'm, I'm driving myself to do something that is, a kind of pushing myself.

6. Deborah

Deborah: I'm, I'm going to talk about walking which I've got into recently, because I'm now commuting into London each day, and I found that I hated the tube so ... so much that I would ... I'm go ... I walk up from Waterloo rail station every day up to work, which is 20 minutes' extremely fast walking. But I like it. It wears down the shoe leather a lot, and I spend a fortune every two weeks on getting my shoes reheeled, but I like it because it's fast, and it's out in the air—which isn't that fresh but at least its better than being in the tube with millions of other people and their polluted air. And, it gets the muscles going. The first week my legs were ... my legs ached terribly but now I'm used to it. It gets the lungs going. It's meant to be the best form of aerobic exercise, if you do it properly. And I think I probably am, because I've got it down to twenty minutes now, erm, which I think, compared with what other people have told me, is quite speedy.

Listening Two

Task a

Three people are giving their opinions about boxing.

Speaker 1: When I look at a picture like this I feel ... hmm ... I feel ... I'm not really sure how I feel.

Interviewer: Disgusted perhaps? Horrified?

Speaker 1: No, no, I wouldn't say that.

Interviewer: Are you excited, perhaps?

Speaker 1: Excited? No, no, not at all. What's there to be excited about?

Interviewer: Well, a lot of people who go to boxing matches seem to be excited.

Speaker 1: Yes, I know. But I really can't understand why anybody should do that sort of thing, at all.

Interviewer: What? Go to a boxing match? Or box in one?

Speaker 1: No, the first. I ... I think ... well ... it's hard to understand why people should want to earn their living by fighting, but I think I can. I mean, it's the money, isn't it? No, I meant going to a thing like that and watching it. I ... I just can't understand it. That's all.

Speaker 2: Well, before ... I used to be disgusted by the idea of this sort of thing. Men fighting for money. Blood. All that sort of thing.

Interviewer: And now?

Speaker 2: Well, since I've started going to a few boxing matches with my boyfriend, I think I see something ... something else in it.

Interviewer: What?

Speaker 2: Well ... perhaps you'll be surprised when I say this ... but I think there's a real element of skill. Yes. Skill.

Interviewer: What kind of skill?

Speaker 2: Physical skill. Those men are really ... fit. And if you watch two good boxers ... boxers who know what they're doing ... you can see the skill. The way they ... they ... the way they watch each other and wait for

	an opening. That sort of thing. It's quite exciting, really. A bit like ... a chess game. Yes.
Speaker 3:	To me it's just disgusting. It's a brutal, disgusting spectacle. It ought to be banned. It sickens me ... the very thought of it sickens me.

Task b

Dad:	Could you pass the crisps, please, Steve? Thanks.
Steve:	Er, Dad, there's something I'd like to ask you, well, tell you really ... (sound of hiccups)
Dad:	Here, Laura, drink this and take some deep breaths ...
Steve:	Dad ...
Dad:	Yes, Steve, I'm listening. Why are you so nervous?
Steve:	Well, I am a bit nervous, I suppose, but it's nothing important really. Er ... it's just that I'd like you to sponsor me in, er, well, something I'm doing. It won't cost much, just a pound. In fact, you can all sponsor me.
Dad:	What are you doing then?
Steve:	Um ... I'm going to do a parachute jump.
Laura:	Parachute jump! How exciting!
Mum:	Are you sure you know what you're doing, Steve?
Dad:	You're not going on a parachute jump, my lad.
Steve:	What do you mean, I'm not going? You can't stop me.
Dad:	Steve, I know you're over 18, but don't you realise that parachuting is extremely dangerous?
Steve:	Oh, come on, Dad, it's not that dangerous. Laura, what do you think?
Laura:	I think it's really fascinating. I want to come, too.
Steve:	Uncle John?
John:	Well, I'm sorry, Steve, but in my opinion, it's a terribly dangerous sport.
Dad:	I quite agree. I mean, it's a skill, and it's not only dangerous, but it's rather expensive, and ...
Steve:	Dad ...
Dad:	And ... I want you to think of your parents for a change.
Steve:	But Dad, listen. There are three points there: one, it's my money—I've earned it; two, you obviously have to do a training course first, so you know exactly what to do when you jump and three, it's sponsored, so it's all in a good cause.
Mum:	Well, in my view, it's an excellent idea, and if I were younger, I'd do it as well. I think you're worrying just a little too much, dear ...

Task c

So, we've already talked a bit about the growth of extreme sports—things like mountain climbing and parachuting. As psychologists, we need to ask ourselves, why is this person doing this? Why do people take these risks and put themselves in danger when they don't have to.

One common trait among risk takers is that they enjoy strong feelings or sensations. We call this trait "sensation seeking". A "sensation seeker" is someone who's always looking for new sensations. What else do we know about sensation seekers?

Well, as I said, sensation seekers like strong emotion. You can see this in many parts of a person's life, not just in extreme sports. For example, many sensation seekers enjoy hard rock music. They like the loud sound and strong emotion of the songs. Similarly, sensation seekers enjoy frightening horror movies. They like the feeling of being scared and horrified while watching the movie. This feeling is even stronger for extreme sports, where the person faces real danger. Sensation seekers feel that danger is very exciting.

In addition, sensation seekers like new experiences that force them to push their personal limits. For them, repeating the same things every day is boring. Many sensation seekers choose jobs that include risk, er, let's see, such as starting a new business, or being an emergency room doctor. These jobs are different every day, so they never know what will happen. That's why many sensation seekers also like extreme sports. When you climb a mountain or jump out of an airplane, you never know what will happen. The activity is always new and different.

Unit 18 Going on Holiday

Listening One

Task b

(Holidays in the United States)

Sandra: So, when do you start your job?
John: Ah, tomorrow, first day tomorrow.
Sandra: Great! You looking forward to it?
John: Well, bit nervous, I suppose.
Sandra: Oh, you'll be all right ... you'll be OK.
John: What about ... what about your holiday? Did you have a good time?

Sandra:	Oh, I just had a wonderful time. Six weeks in the States ... California.
John:	I went to the States.
Sandra:	You didn't! Where?
John:	I went to ... on the east side, New York, Washington, Boston and then I went up North to the Great Lakes ... just beautiful, just wonderful.
Sandra:	No, I was the other side. I went to California as I said ... 'cos I've got cousins there, and we went to New Orleans, Disneyworld, oh ... just had such a fantastic time ... My cousins are crazy on sailing, you see, and I'm mad on it, too ... and we did surfing and windsurfing and ... we're just all sea maniacs, our family.
John:	Incredible! You're lucky to have people to stay with ... I ... er ... had to ... well, I was camping or staying in Youth Hostels. I had friends in New York I stayed with, which ... helped a great ... 'cos New York's so expensive.
Sandra:	I can imagine ... I've never been, but ...
John:	I just ... getting into all the museums and things ... the Metropolitan and the Whiteworth Gallery ... just ... well, just going up to the top of the Empire State Building ... all costs money ... everything ... terribly expensive.
Sandra:	I'd love to go one year. It was worth going, wasn't it?
John:	Oh, just wonderful ... incredible, yes, all of it, and I went to a couple of concerts, too ... rock concerts ... they were ...
Sandra:	Gosh ... were they expensive ... yeah, they were expensive?
John:	Oh, wow, yes, but great.
Sandra:	Oh, I was just so lucky. I was wined and dined by my cousins, and it was great ... and the food they gave me was just fantastic ... lot of fresh fish and things ... from the fishing ... ah!
John:	I had to live off hamburgers and hot dogs ...
Sandra:	You poor thing!
John:	I couldn't afford to eat in the posh restaurants or anything like that ... Oh so, work for you tomorrow, eh?
Sandra:	Yes ... afraid so ... I can't face it really. I just want to go to the States ... to the good life.

Task c

Ellen:	Hey, Jim! Hi! How are things going?
Jim:	Just fine, Ellen, how are you?
Ellen:	Oh, I'm just fine. What can I do for you?

Jim: Well, I've got to go to Miami next month and I'd like you to make the arrangements.

Ellen: Wonderful! When do you want to go?

Jim: OK, I have to be there from the sixth through the ninth of February.

Ellen: OK ... sixth through the ninth. (Right.) Now, the sixth is a Thursday. Do you know, if you could leave on a Friday, the seventh, before noon, I could get you a special weekend fare for three hundred forty-nine dollars round trip? (Oh?) Now, that's a real saving. The regular fare is five thirty-five. Uh, you'd have to return on that Sunday, the ninth.

Jim: Uh ... what time would I get into Miami on the Seventh?

Ellen: Mm, just a sec ... the only flight that's open leaves Detroit at ten-fifteen a.m. and arrives in Miami at one o'clock.

Jim: Is that a direct flight?

Ellen: Oh yes. That's a non-stop Detroit–Miami.

Jim: Hmm ... I really should be there the night before. (Mm.) Ellen, what about other specials?

Ellen: OK, well, there's a seven-day excursion fare that's cheaper. That means you have to go for seven or more days (Uh-huh.) and you have to fly on weekdays, Monday through Thursday. That's three hundred twenty-four dollars round trip.

Jim: When does that flight leave?

Ellen: Uh, that flight leaves daily at noon and arrives in Miami at three forty-five.

Jim: Is that a non-stop flight?

Ellen: No, that one isn't a non-stop. There's a one-hour stopover in Atlanta, but you don't have to change planes, at least.

Jim: What about the return flight to Detroit on the seven-day excursion fare?

Ellen: OK. Let me check ... Right. That's a daily, Monday through Thursday, flight. The departure time from Miami is three p.m. arrives in Detroit at six forty-five.

Jim: You know, it might be possible for me to stay in Miami a whole week, because I have a lot of friends down there. Uh, that seven-day excursion is the cheapest way.

Ellen: Yeah, it's a great rate. Oh, there is one other, the night flight, two hundred ninety-nine dollars. Now, that leaves at eleven p.m., stops in Atlanta, and arrives in Miami at two forty-five in the morning.

Jim: No red-eye specials for me, thank you! (OK.) I tell you, I've got to think that over and I'll call you tomorrow.

Ellen:	OK. That'll be fine. Oh, with the weekend special, I can get you a good inexpensive hotel room downtown.
Jim:	No, that's OK. I got someplace to stay. But I do need a car, so can you check into car rentals and, uh, you can make all the arrangements at the same time?
Ellen:	Fine. I'll have all the information ready for you.
Jim:	Thanks, Ellen. You're great! I'll be in touch.
Ellen:	Very good. Thanks. Thanks, Jim, for dropping by.

Listening Two

Task a

(Stephen Taylor is a famous canoeist. He has just returned to England after an amazing journey in his canoe. He went to some friends to one of the highest mountains in Africa, and three of them came down the mountain side by canoe on one of the rivers. The journey down the mountain took 5 days. The canoeists took a camera with them and made a film of their amazing trip. When Stephen arrived at London airport after the adventure. A radio reporter was waiting for him.)

Reporter:	Congratulations, Mr. Taylor. How does it feel to be home?
Stephen:	Wonderful. It's a warm day, too.
Reporter:	Was it very cold in the mountains?
Stephen:	It was very cold on the first day. If you see the film on television, you'll see what I mean. There were blocks of ice floating in the river. Some of them were bigger than I am.
Reporter:	Isn't that very dangerous?
Stephen:	Yes, it is. The ice is moving all the time. The pieces are enormous and they bang into each other. I kept thinking, "If one of those hits me, it will kill me." Apart from that, ice can make holes in big ships, so you can imagine what happens if a sharp piece of ice hits a canoe.
Reporter:	What was the most dangerous part of the journey?
Stephen:	I don't really know. On the second day we came to a part of the river which is very narrow. There are sheer rockfaces on each side of the river, and the water moves between them very quickly. That was very dangerous. If you fall into water like that, it will kill you in two minutes.
Reporter:	Because the water is so fast?
Stephen:	Yes, and because it's so cold. There's no ice in that part of the river, but

	the water is almost freezing. The cold alone will kill you very quickly.
Reporter:	But you had some friends on the ground beside the river, didn't you?
Stephen:	Yes. Three of us came down the river in the canoes, and three people walked down the mountain. They carried the heavy things—food, tents and extra clothes.
Reporter:	And they were there to help you? They had a radio, didn't they?
Stephen:	Yes, we had an aeroplane waiting at the bottom of the mountain. It was the same aeroplane that took us to the top of the river. But for the first three days we only saw the walkers in the morning and the evening.
Reporter:	Why?
Stephen:	The canoes were travelling much too quickly. We couldn't stop, and the walkers couldn't walk quickly enough. And when we came to the narrow part of the river, they were on the top of the cliff and the river was at the bottom. They couldn't help us at all.
Reporter:	But you didn't have any accidents?
Stephen:	Not there, luckily. On the third day we came to a little waterfall, just before the small lake. One of my friends fell out of his canoe.
Reporter:	What happened to him?
Stephen:	He managed to swim to the side, but he lost his canoe. He walked down the mountain with the others.
Reporter:	He wasn't hurt?
Stephen:	No. The only serious accident happened on the land later that day. One of the walkers fell over, and broke his leg. The aeroplane came and took him to hospital. We didn't know about it until afterwards. We were in our canoes on the other side of the lake.
Reporter:	And the aeroplane took the man away?
Stephen:	Yes. Luckily he was beside the lake. The land is flat there, and the aeroplane was able to land. That taught me something. If I ever do anything like this again, I'll take a helicopter, not a plane. Then, if there is an accident in the mountains, there won't be any difficulty. A helicopter can always get to you, even if it can't land.
Reporter:	Which part of the journey will you remember most?
Stephen:	Oh, the last two days, I think. We left the lake and went down the river. It was wider and slower, and it was much easier to manage the canoes. The scenery was beautiful. I'd like to spend a week going down that part of the river.
Reporter:	You'd like to go back?

Recording Script

Stephen: Yes, I would. In fact, if I can find another team of canoeists, I'll go back next summer and make another film.

Reporter: Thank you, Mr. Taylor.

Task b

Announcer: You're listening to Radio Europe International. Welcome to our International Tourist Service, supplied by the tourist boards of France, Holland, Belgium, Germany and Switzerland. Listen in to this program every day to find out what's on where to make the most of your holiday.

If you're interested in tradition and folklore, then today there are traditional games and dancing being held in the Vondel park in Amsterdam. These start at 2:00 p.m.

For those who enjoy exhibitions, there's plenty to keep you busy. At the Louvre in Paris an Impressionist exhibition starts today and will continue for the next fortnight. The Palais des Beaux Arts in Brussels is in the middle of a month-long Picasso exhibition, and in Stuttgart there is an exhibition with a difference: an exhibition of traditional German food, with plenty to eat, of course. So, if you like your food or if you're hungry, why not head for Stuttgart Town Hall from 10:00 a.m. onwards?

Sports lovers also have a fine choice today with a yachting regatta beginning at 11:00 a.m.—wind permitting—from Geneva on Lake Geneva, International Athletics Championships in the sports stadium in Amsterdam, and canoeing events on the Rhine at Weisbaden. And finally for this evening, most places have a long list of concerts and theatre. See Bruce Springsteen, for example, at Fyenoord Football Stadium in Rotterdam or a classical concert in the open air—the National Orchestra of France playing Beethoven's fifth symphony—in the Bois de Boulogne in Paris at 9:00 p.m.

There's much more available, of course. Should you require extra information, why not call Radio Europe International's Tourist Information Centre. The number is 033-207632. I'll say that number again: 033-207632. And if you need information about children's activities ring 033-207633. We'll repeat this service in five minutes in case you didn't catch any of the information you're interested in.

This is the International Tourist Service of Radio Europe International wishing you a very enjoyable day.

Task d

A: It is a gorgeous, sunny day, and I'm here in the mountains. I have with me Tom Davis, who is the chief of the Mountain Rescue Service here. Tom, many of our viewers will be thinking of hiking in the mountains this summer. Do you have any advice for them?

B: Yes, Tracy, I sure do. Uh ... You know, most ... uh ... emergency rescues are easily avoidable if ... if you take the right precautions before and during your hike, and if you take the right equipment with you.

A: Oh, that's good to hear. Why don't you tell us about the precautions first?

B: All right. Uh ... here are ten important dos and don'ts ...

A: Oh, you ... you've got a little list there.

B: Absolutely. Number one. Have at least 4 people in your party. Don't go hiking alone.

A: Good advice.

B: Mm-hmm. Number two. Expect the weather to get worse; don't rely completely on weather forecasts, especially the ones in newspapers.

A: Yeah, except for ours, of course. Our channel, you rely on that one. (Ah, absolutely.) Right.

B: Of course. Uh ... three. Allow yourself plenty of time; don't let darkness catch up with you.

A: OK.

B: Uh ... Number four would be to walk at the pace of the slowest member of your group. Don't leave anyone behind.

A: Yeah, that would be me.

B: OK, in your case...

A: Don't leave me behind.

B: OK, I won't.

A: OK.

B: Five, Before you start off, tell people where you're going; don't forget to tell them when you get back.

A: OK, great advice, Tom! Thank you. How about the essential equipment? Um ... Oh, nothing too heavy, I hope.

B: No, no, no, you need a good backpack. And that brings me to ... to point Number six. You have to plan your route before you set off; Take a map and a compass so that you ... uh ... you know where you are at all times during the hike.

A: OK.

B: Uh ... Seven, in your backpack you want to carry some warm, water-proof clothing, and also remember to take a first-aid kit.

A: Right.

B: Eight, wear proper hiking boots—not sneakers ... or ... sandals.

A: OK.

B: Uh ... Number nine. Uh ... Put emergency rations in your backpack, like chocolate, ... uh ... dried fruit, and ... and ... water, as well as any sandwiches and drinks you need during the day. And, finally, Number ten. Pack a flashlight in case you get caught in the dark.

A: Oh, my, I hope not!

B: Oh, don't worry—usually everything goes fine, and everyone has a great time. You just have to be prepared.

A: OK, thanks, Tom. I think I'll go home and start to plan my trip for ... uh ... next year!

B: See you on the peak.

A: OK.

Reference Key to Listening Tasks

Unit 1 Personal Information

Listening One

Task b

Full name:	Alice (Mary) Saunders
Present job:	hotel receptionist
Date of birth:	7th Oct. 1963
Marital status:	single
Address:	9 Worthington Street, London, NW10
Telephone No.:	2744011

Task c

name:	What's your name?
present job:	What do you do at the moment?
date of birth:	May I have your date of birth?
marital status:	Are you married or single?
address:	May I have your address?

Task d

Name:	Isabel Martinez
Age:	22
Occupation:	student
Nationality:	Spain
UK Address:	Youth Hostel, High Street
Length of course:	4 weeks

Reference Key to Listening Tasks

Number of hours per day:	3
Course starting date:	July 15th
Price of course plus accommodation:	600 pounds
Accommodation:	required
Amount of deposit paid:	20 pounds
School facilities:	TV and video room, cookery and pottery classes, tennis courts, swimming pool, library
Teachers:	good, well trained teachers

Listening Two

Task b

When people meet, they usually
1. talk about something they have in common
2. say their names
3. ask more questions

Task c

	Strategies to Make a Good First Impression
1.	Try to remember people's names by using them.
2.	Try to add information. Don't just say yes or *no*.
3.	Try to find something that's the same for both of you.
4.	Think about what you want to say.

Unit 2 You and Me

Listening One

Task b

1st Speaker: a nice meal; to go to Indonesia; getting to Oxford University; Winston Churchill; his wife; daughter said he was wonderful

2nd Speaker: reading a book in front of a fire; to have enough money; having her daughter; Gandhi; her daughter; went for a nice walk

3rd Speaker: his work; to go on a safari in East Africa; raising three daughters; his wife; his wife; went for a drive out in the country

Task c

David: professional baseball player; read (the classics); had 1st baby; his wife; be a father of five

Suzanne: lawyer; run (jog); ran in Boston Marathon; Martin Luther King, Jr.; win Boston Marathon

Adolfo: dancer; watch musicals (movies); moved to U.S.; Sophia Loren; still dancing

Linda: goes to beauty school; hang out with friends; went to a Bruce Springsteen concert; his father (dad); have her own beauty school

Listening Two

Task b

Questions	Martin	Robert	Jean
1.	not particularly important, big family important	most important things in life	
2.		someone with common interest, and is often silent	someone who you can count on, who can help you and listen to your problems
3.		not always	yes, very often

Task c

1. how long they've been there
2. where they live/come from
3. the boy's trip round the world
4. windsurfing
5. going to supper at the girl's house

Reference Key to Listening Tasks

Unit 3 City and Country

Listening One

Task b

advantages of living in a village:
- friendly people
- healthy life
- less crime
- cheaper accommodation
- fresh air
- safe
- less traffic
- quiet and peaceful

advantages of living in a large city:
- more entertainment
- stores and shops
- traffic more convenient
- open-minded people
- opportunity to make new friends

Task d

Names	Ben	Janice
Opinion of city	exciting, noisy, dirty	exciting
Opinion of tourist sites	amazing, especially the skyscrapers	prefers the monument, the Statue of Liberty beautiful
Opinion of taxis	not too bad	expensive
Opinion of subways	it's all right, cheap	hates it—terribly dirty
Opinion of hotels	awful—prefers older hotels	likes it
Name and address of hotel	Hotel Metropolitan 103 East 49th Street	

Listening Two

Task b

Plane
— Cost: $130 one way, $260 round trip (903/1807 francs)

— Advantages: quick, convenient (10-11 flights/day)
— Disadvantages: have to get to the airport in Paris and from the airport in Frankfurt (adds 3 extra hours); expensive

Train
— Cost: $50 one way (second class), $98 round trip (338/676 francs)
— Advantages: inexpensive, beautiful trip, comfortable, arrives in centre of Frankfurt
— Disadvantages: takes 6 hours, only 3 direct trains a day (not so convenient)

Bus
— Cost: (doesn't say)
— Advantages: (doesn't say)
— Disadvantages: have to change buses several times, long trip (13 hours)

Car
— Cost: $35 a day (240 francs)
— Advantages: can pick own route, scenic trip, would have car to use in Frankfurt
— Disadvantages: long, tiring drive (7-8 hours)

Unit 4 Marriage

Listening One

Task b

1. George Hayes—ideal wife: short, brown eyes, happy face
2. Fenella Orchard—ideal husband: tall, thin, grey hair, blue eyes
3. Stella Richards—ideal husband: a beard, glasses, short
4. Albert Winterton-ideal wife: tall, thin, blue eyes, blond hair

Task d

Bachelor 1
— vice-president of Ace Construction Company
— gambling, driving sports car, dating beautiful women

Reference Key to Listening Tasks

— good-looking, intelligent, ambitious, witty, rich

— (No answer given.)

Bachelor 2

— composer

— entertaining a wonderful woman at home, playing the piano and singing songs for her

— a good listener, interested in other people

— staying up all night and sleeping during the day

Bachelor 3

— airline pilot

— doing outdoor activities, skiing, hiking, playing tennis, cycling

— dependable, reliable

— having a quick temper

Listening Two

Task a

	Information
Her first husband	hard-working, sociable, not enough money, lovely considerate, fun to be with
Her first marriage	husband killed in the train crash
Her second husband	good looking, jobless, does no housework, untidy, likes drinking, violent, unfaithful
Her second marriage	divorce with her husband
Her third husband	ideal husband, has a good job, does housework, doesn't drink much, good with the children
Her third marriage	a happy marriage

Task c

1. Not sure.
2. She was still seeing an old boyfriend of hers.
3. She did not share his religious views.
4. He prefers to marry only the right person.

Task d

Marriage Customs	
Chinese Customs over the Years	Traditional Hopi Culture
Marriage partners were chosen by parents or older family members. Parents used matchmakers. Young people make their own choices.	Boys visited girls late at night. After the girl became pregnant, the couple got married.

Unit 5 Keep in Touch

Listening One

Task b

Message 1: Mary Roberts from the First National Bank asks you to call her at 772-1852 before 12:30, or between 2:00 and 5:00 this afternoon.

Message 2: Mr. Brown has to cancel lunch appointment. Please call to reschedule: 743-9821.

Message 3: Your wife won't be home till 8—working late.

Message 4: Wendy from Travel Agents International called. You're booked on Pan Am flight 226 to Puerto Rico on Tuesday the 12th at 8 a.m. Sending ticket over this afternoon.

Message 5: Juan Salvador called about meeting next Wed. Will call back.

Task c

Who Is the Speaker Talking to?	What Are They Talking About?
1. a garage mechanic	Misunderstanding about the car being repaired. Caller was talking about a red care, and mechanic was talking about an orange one.
2. a strange woman	A case of mistaken identity. The caller phoned the wrong Mark Smith, and spoke with his wife who was suspicious.
3. a co-worker	Another woman they both work with in the office who seems to feel that she can order the other two around. This really irritates the caller and her friend.
4. his girlfriend	They had a fight last night; the man was jealous and is calling to apologise.

Reference Key to Listening Tasks

Listening Two

Task a

1. Letter to J. O'Brien—she gets the job in Jeddah.
2. Letter to J. Ryan—failed.
3. Phone Nursing Weekly: i. mistake in Kuwait ad.; ii. placing ad. for Dental Nurse.
4. Ask Jim to fix heater and washbasin.
5. Buy some coffee.
6. Water the plants.

Task b

1. Note for Mr. Donaldson
   James Smith is coming to see you on Friday at 12:15.
2. Note for Professor Freedom
   Richard Jones is coming to see you on Thursday at 9:45.
3. Note for Dr. Nelson
   Anne Brown is coming to see you on Wednesday at 2:40.
4. Note for Mrs. Harper
   David Sim is coming to see you on Tuesday at 4:20.

Task c

	Speaker A	Speaker B	Topic or Purpose of Conversation
1.	shop-assistant	customer	trying to get a refund
2.	former pupil	school master	trying to get Mr. T. to remember him
3.	mother	daughter	trying to persuade her to eat
4.	spy	spy	arranging meeting and signal
5.	student	student	talking about homework
6.	male stranger	woman in cafe	trying to pick her up (or just being friendly)

Unit 6 Habits

Listening One

Task b

1. I don't make the bed.
2. I read—sometimes.
3. Not very untidy (his side of the bed).
4. Try to think of sometimes else.
5. Only if somebody comes to the door or the telephone rings.
6. I'd go down and have a look around.
7. No.
8. I don't dream very much.

Task c

6. Wait to see if it happens again. Would get up eventually.
4. I lie awake and think about things
2. Clean my teeth; read a bit
8. Worrying dreams
1. No time at all
7. Take up quite a lot of room

Task d

> The woman is tired all day.
> Sleep deprivation is very serious. We get cranky and our job performance is poor. We might have an accident.
> — A ship accident (The Exxon Valdez)
> — Care crashes
> — The woman is tired and cranky, and doesn't make good decisions about parenting or her health.
> — By Friday she's not a safe driver.

Reference Key to Listening Tasks

Listening Two

Task a

Steve:	about 16; family smoked; to be grown up; friends smoked
Miriam:	18; socially; everybody smoked; to be grown up
Anne:	first year at university; everybody smoked; social habit
John:	at school; other children gave him cigarettes; fashionable, sophisticated, adult

Task b

1. Liz: was pregnant
2. Miriam: to save money
3. Alison: had flu, sore throat or laryngitis
4. Anne: was pregnant
5. Muriel: had nasty taste in mouth
6. Cecil: painful to do sports
7. Miriam: in love with a non-smoker

Unit 7 Clubs/Societies

Listening One

Task b

Name:	Video Club
Number of present members:	80
Began in:	1981
Objectives:	1) rent films on video and show them
	2) make their own films
	3) make a short magazine-type program each week
Membership fee:	free
Rights of members:	can use all the equipment of the club, only pay for video tapes

Task c

1. Historical Society

Objectives:	to provide a meeting place for students interested in historical subjects
Locations/Times of meetings:	every other Thursday; in the Junior Common Room on F staircase
Past record:	explored history of the town and famous former inhabitants; visited several historical houses in the area
Plans:	to go out more to visit historical sites and locations

2. Pop Music Society

Objectives:	to spread the knowledge and awareness of all types of modern music
Locations/Times of meetings:	Friday evening; in the stereo room
Past record:	built up a large library of LPs, cassettes and videos; organised several concerts at college by local bands
Plans:	to increase the number of bands they can attract from other parts of the country; to organise more bookings to big concerts in major venues

3. The Players

Objectives:	to put on one play a term
Locations/Times of meetings:	as often as possible in the large assembly room in F Block
Past record:	performed two plays; arranged visits to the theatre; arranged visits from famous actors
Plans:	to present plays by living authors; to arrange more visits from actors

Reference Key to Listening Tasks

Listening Two

Task b

Notes about the Sports Center

Membership fee:	£9.50 a year
Where to register:	reception
Time to register:	Monday to Thursday, 2 to 6
What to bring for registration:	Union card, passport photo and fee
Opening hours:	9 a.m. to 10 p.m. weekdays and from 10 a.m. to 6 p.m. on Saturdays
Hours for 50 percent discount:	9 a.m. to 12 noon on weekdays
Facility 1:	the Main Hall
For which sports:	football, volleyball and basketball, badminton and aerobics
Facility 2:	the dance studio
For which sports:	ballet, modern dance and martial arts
Other facilities and arrangement:	squash courts (six of them), fitness room, arrangement with the local tennis club

Unit 8 Past Schooling

Listening One

Task b

Questions	Jack	Shirley
1.	homesick at aunt's house at the seaside	Lake District: honey and porridge for breakfast
2.	wanted to take his toys	very frightened and shy
3.	No, wasn't a good student & teachers didn't seem to like him	Yes. Felt sorry when holidays came

(Continued)

4.	Miss Robson—kind marvellous story-teller	Miss Brown—made history come to life
5.	Mr. Goodman—used to pull his ear	Mrs. Sharpe—impatient math teacher
6.	Bucket of water fell on Mr. Goodman	She cried and sang her favorite hymns.

Task d

The way they looked: Curtis: hair down to his waist; Grace: flower painted on face; Martin: wore blue jeans with lots of holes in them

Their worst memory: Driving home for spring break and running out of gas when all the gas stations were closed. They tried to get gas from a gas pump and the neighbors called the police. Almost got arrested.

Their best memory: Getting arrested with 500 other students at a peace demonstration.

Last day of college: They didn't go to the graduation ceremony and went on a picnic instead.

Listening Two

Task a

1. He refused to sit down and went round the classroom knocking all the other kids onto the floor.
2. She felt very frightened.
3. Because she was so bad at it.
4. He thinks the most important thing is to be taught how to think and analyze things.
5. Because there are so few jobs.

Reference Key to Listening Tasks

Unit 9 Past and Future

Listening One

Task a

1. Simon
   a. ... at the turn of the century from Poland.
   b. ... 10 years.
   c. ... had been living in great poverty.

2. Ronda
   a. For 4 generations.
   b. In the south-west of England.
   c. They had been having a pretty hard time of it.
   d. When he was a lad/on a business trip to Sydney.
   e. Her father upped and moved to where they live now.

3. Alistair
   a. To William the Conqueror's time.
   b. His grandparents did it.
   c. Because the costs and the discomfort were becoming too great for him.
   d. ... he had tried to sell it and failed.
   e. Alistair and his family have been living in the 17 bedroom house.

4. Caroline
   a. She had been living in the south of France.
   b. At a gala ball at the Casino.
   c. She'd spilt all the things out of her basket and as she was picking them up, she looked up and saw "this most gorgeous man."

Listening Two

Task a

1. apartments, lettuce, water, soap, beef, fuel
2. 50%

3. It's hot all the time.

4. soylent red, yellow (made from soybeans) and soylent green (from ocean plants)

5. the man

Task d

d

Unit 10 Commercials/Advertisements

Listening One

Task a

	Name	Effect
Ad. 1	Thief Buster	Security system to protect your car
Ad. 2	Rinse Away	Hair shampoo, a cure for dandruff

Task b

1. Clensip is just ordinary water.

2. Packaging ideas—Clensip in bottles and cans;

Slogans: "It's Clensip, naturally it's good for you."; "Be different, drink Clensip!"; "Drink Clensip, the non-fattening drink in a can."

A picture: Lots of girls in red—one girl in white drinking Clensip.

Another picture: Lots of young men in sailing boats—one young man in a white suit is in a big yacht drinking Clensip.

3.
— drink it
— wash hair in it
— wash face in it
— bathe eyes

Reference Key to Listening Tasks

   — soak feet
   — clean floors
   — cook
4. pure, natural, clean, clear, healthy, non-fattening, refreshing, soothing

Listening Two

Task a

	Employee Complaint
Employee's name	Anthony Morgan
Position	Advertising copywriter
Subject of complaint	text for a video advertising a hotel
Complaint	Text does not give an honest report about what hotel is like.
Reasons given	Tony Morgan went to stay there last year, and it was a terrible hotel.
Result of meeting	Tony has a chance to rewrite parts of the script.

Task b

1) has to be seen to be believed
2) first impression
3) two crowded
4) quite clean
5) remarkable
6) waiters
7) only just cooked
8) Nobody knows
9) have to eat
10) right back to the kitchen
11) Perhaps
12) comfortable
13) can
14) no
15) will
16) are
17) clean
18) hot
19) ask
20) If
21) forget
22) surprise you

Unit 11 Entertainment

Listening One

Task a

The Empire Strikes Back Theater: Westside Cinema Times: 7:10, 9:45 Ticket price: $5	*Casablanca* Theater: Metro Times: 9:10 Ticket price: $4
Rocky III Theater: Circle Theater Times: 7:05, 9:30 Ticket price:/	*Kramer vs. Kramer* Theater: Palace Times: 8:00 Ticket price: $2.50

John—

We're going to see <u>Casablanca</u> at <u>9:00</u> p.m. at the <u>Metro</u> Theater. Meet us at the Sunset Bar and Grill (across the street) at <u>8:00</u> p.m. or outside the theater at <u>9:00</u>.

Task b

1. *Casablanca*: old film, fantastic, made in the 40's, wartime drama, brilliant
2. *Rambo*: revolting, gratuitous violence, terrible
3. *Psycho*: great, old, a thriller, brilliant
4. *E.T.*: sweet, a real tear jerker
5. *Chariots of Fire*: music, dull
6. *Godfather*: gory, frightening, old

Listening Two

Task b

1) old Dutch   2) 7:50
3) 16   4) variety show
5) band   6) cartoons
7) 10:15   8) news
9) Keeping Fit   10) movie

Reference Key to Listening Tasks

Unit 12 Climate and Weather

Listening One

Task a

(Reference words for exercise)

dry	rain	rainy	temperature
wet	moisture	damp	humid
hot	warm	stuffy	windy
cool	chilly	fine	freezing
sunny	overcast	snow	sleet
shower	drizzle	gale	downpour
mist	breeze	frost	hurricane
hail	thunder	icy	thunderstorm
fog	lightning	blizzard	snowstorm
windstorm	tornado	hazy	

Task b

Chicago:	cloudy, rain, colder, high temperature 45 degrees, lower temperature 32 degrees
San Francisco:	showers
Los Angeles:	fair, low seventies
Denver:	cold & windy, 38 degrees, 30 miles/an hour wind
Dallas:	cold, 48
Toronto:	rain, maybe snow
Montreal:	heavy snow
Miami:	clear skies, sunny, 78 degreesT

ask c

Britain:	24 degrees, warm day, hazy sunshine
Sweden:	cold, 15 degrees, heavy rain
France:	showers, hazy sunshine, 25 degrees
Spain:	warm, dry, 30 degrees
Italy:	lots of sunshine/sunny, hotter, 33 degrees
Greece:	thunderstorms, cooler, 25 degrees

243

Southern Mediterranean: extremely hot, 35 degrees, cloudy to clear
Switzerland: snow, freezing, 0 degree

Listening Two

Task a

Seattle: rain, 50 degrees
San Diego: sunny, 78 degrees
Oklahoma City: sunny, 65 degrees
Houston: cloudy, 69 degrees
Miami: cloudy and windy, 64 degrees
New York: heavy rains, high winds, cold temperatures, 35 degrees
Montreal: snow flurries, 28 degrees
Toronto: sunny, 30 degrees

Unit 13 Accommodation

Listening One

Task a

(Reference words for Exercise)
in a living room:

wallpaper	carpet	rug
curtains (drapes)	mat	fireplace
bookcase	coffee table	radiator

in a bedroom:

dressing table	wardrobe	double bed
single bed	cupboard (closet)	
chest of drawers	sheets	blanket
pillows	quilt	bedside table

Reference Key to Listening Tasks

in a kitchen:
sink	dishwasher	refrigerator
draining board	washing machine	automatic kettle
oven	cooker	

in a bathroom:
washbasin	bath (tub)	toilet
shower	taps (faucets)	toilet tissue

Task b

bathroom:	fully fitted
bed-sitting room:	dining room table and chairs, foldaway double bed, mattress, armchair, fitted wardrobes, sofa, roller blinds, coffee tables
kitchen:	washing machine, tumble dryer, electric cooker, refrigerator

Task c

hall:	nice, little, with a telephone point
east-facing room:	nice, big, lovely, big windows, a power point on the wall, no central heating
west-facing room:	dark, wallpaper not good
kitchen:	not bad, built-in cupboards, plenty of power points, modern sink-unit, nice and big windows which look onto the garden
garden:	a typical lawn
dining room:	very handy, small but nice
location of the house:	next to the bus stop, shops and doctor convenient
staircase:	steep
bedrooms:	nice, lovely long view from windows, pleasant decoration
single bedroom:	tiny, plenty of room for a single bed
bathroom:	nice, dark blue tiles, blue bath, thick, white carpet

Listening Two

Task b

1. TV: in corner of room
2. radio: on nightstand by bed

3. restaurant: 2nd floor

4. coffee shop: lobby

5. shops: nearby

6. hairdresser and newsstand: off the lobby to the right of the desk

7. room service: call on phone

8. revolving cocktail lounge: top floor

9. swimming pool: basement

10. sauna: basement

Unit 14 Stay Well

Listening One

Task a

(Reference words for Exercise)

unfit	overweight	weak	fit
slim	energetic	active	strong
muscular	ill	sick	unwell
dizzy	healthy	drug	pill
tablet	lotion	ointment	drops
injection	bandage	plaster	operation
disease	infection	flu	measles
fever	sore throat	pain	nervous breakdown
ache	heart attack	insomnia	allergy
cut	food poisoning	swelling	bruise
toothache	headache		

Task b

1. bad back; rest and sleep (on hard mattress)

2. injured wrist; go to hospital for an X-ray

3. smoker's cough; give up cigarettes

4. trouble with sleep; hot drink with whisky, mild sleeping pills

Task c

1. not sleeping well; get more ex., drink a little hot milk with brandy
2. backache; use a heating pad, put a board under mat., do back ex.
3. burned finger; put ice cube on it
4. sore throat; drink hot water with honey and lemon juice, drink hot tea, stop smoking so much

Listening Two

Task b

Patients	Major Symptoms	Treatments	Possible Illness
1.	Chills, upset stomach, stuffy nose	Bed rest, nasal spray, drink fluids	Flu
2.	Rash, itching	Skin cream, no touching	Poison oak/ivy
3.	Indigestion	Visit doctor, antacid	Upset stomach

Unit 15 What's My Line?

Listening One

Task b

Age:	19
Qualifications:	school qualifications, certificates for ballet and playing the piano
Interests:	music, dancing, animals, tennis, swimming, meeting people
Personality:	none
Organisational ability:	disorganised
Intelligence:	bright, reasonably intelligent
Attitude to work:	lazy
Appearance:	looks very nice

Task d

Questions	Applicant One	Applicant Two
1.	Yours is the biggest company, may offer the biggest opportunities.	A bit bored with present job, would like a change, yours is a bigger company, with better salary, flexible time.
2.	No weakness. Has ambition, flexible and reliable.	A sense of humor; disorganized, a bit late, reliable, says what he's going to do.
3.	Knows a lot about system support, this seems to be a perfect job.	Got the right qualifications, interested, likes a challenge, quite independent.
4.	To progress within the organization, more responsibility, more money.	Australia, a hot and sunny place, may feel like another change after a couple of years.
5.	19,000 plus overtime, 22,000 altogether, has a pension scheme.	Keeps the weekends completely free, wants to go to Scotland and play sports.

Listening Two

Task a

Speaker A

His job: waiter in a bar

What he enjoys: the hours (working at night); being around people and listening to their problems

What he dislikes: the noise, smelling like cigarettes at the end of the night

Speaker B

Her job: dance teacher

What she enjoys: being active; picking out the music for her classes; educating people about their bodies; showing people how to do exercise safely; seeing students make progress; being able to eat what she wants and not gain weight

What she dislikes: hard to come up with new ideas and routines for classes; having to yell

Speaker C

His job: artist

What he enjoys: making money; the creativity of the job; his studio; his tools; the variety

What he dislikes: the pressure; working against a deadline; the business end (contracting clients, negotiating contracts)

Speaker D
Her job: accountant
What she enjoys: working with figures and money; it's fun when the company is making money
What she dislikes: paying the bills; having to remember when bills and taxes are due (the pressure); lots of reading

Task b

Information Card

Name: J.V. Brown   Male
Age: 45
Occupation: Plumber
Description: Short, fat, bearded, bald
Possible jobs: Several answers are possible

Unit 16 Making Your Point

Listening One

Task b

Expert	Opinion	Reason
Donald Sterling	Against it	Spanking teaches children to be violent. It starts a cycle of violence that the child will pass on to his or her children.
Phyllis Jones	For it in some cases	Spanking is effective if done in the context of a loving home.
Lois Goldin	For it	Children need discipline because the number of crimes committed by children and teens is increasing.

Task c

> ### Lecture Notes
>
> *Lecture Topic*: computer ethics
>
> *Definition of an ethical action*: something that someone does that benefits someone and doesn't hurt anyone
>
> *The goal of Computer Ethics Institute*: to increase awareness of the ethical issues that are likely to come up as technology develops
>
> *# 1 Commandment*: Don't use a computer to harm other people.
>
> *# 2 Commandment*: Don't interfere with other people's computer work.
>
> *# 3 Commandment*: Don't snoop in other people's files.
>
> *# 4 Commandment*: Don't use a computer to steal.
>
> *# 5 Commandment*: Don't use a computer to say things that are untrue.
>
> *# 6 Commandment*: Don't use software for which you have not paid.
>
> *# 7 Commandment*: Don't use other people's computer resources without telling or without paying them.
>
> *# 8 Commandment*: Don't appropriate someone else's ideas.
>
> *# 9 Commandment*: Think about the social consequences of the program you are writing.
>
> *# 10 Commandment*: Always use a computer in ways that are respectful of others.

Listening Two

Task a

1. Speakers:	a customer and a sales clerk
The customer's problem:	The recorder he bought from the shop was defective to begin with and has ruined several of his tapes.
The clerk's arguments:	Warranty expired 10 days ago, so she has no obligation to fix the machine for free. Rules are rules.
2. Speakers:	A husband and his wife
The husband's problem:	He doesn't do his part of the housework.
The wife's arguments:	The husband should do his cleaning without being told. That's his responsibility. She does her cleaning even when

Reference Key to Listening Tasks

                              she's tired after a busy day at work.

3. Speakers: An employee and his employer

The employee's problem: He can't live on current salary and therefore wants a pay raise.

The employer's arguments: The company gives raises only to merit; otherwise it would go out of business. The employee hasn't shown enough enthusiasm or initiative.

Task b

Reasons for capital punishment:

— If someone kills, he or she should die.

— The death penalty will scare people and stop them from killing (a deterrent).

— Prisons are crowded.

— The taxpayer has to pay to keep these hardened criminals in prison.

— Criminals are never really rehabilitated.

— Some people are just bad.

Reasons against capital punishment:

— No one, not even the government, has the right to take human life.

— The death penalty doesn't prevent killer from killing.

— Some people sentenced to death aren't guilty.

— We should be rehabilitating criminals, not killing them.

— The real problem is a social one—poverty, drugs discrimination.

Unit 17 Sports

Listening One

Task a

(Reference words for Exercise)

athlete	player	rider	contestant
referee	umpire	supporter (fan)	field
court	course	ground	ring

track	stadium	beat	draw
table tennis	basketball	race	dash
swimming	diving	cycling	yachting
canoeing	football	rugby	soccer
shooting	skiing	skating	badminton
boxing	judo	wrestling	hurdling
weight lifting	Marathon	rowing	

Task b

1. Alison: swimming
2. Susanna: mixture of aerobics, yoga and stretch exercise
3. Tim: weight-training
4. Iain: amateur athletics (track running)
5. Bridget: yoga
6. Deborah: walking

Listening Two

Task a

1. Can't understand why people go and watch boxing matches. The boxers are simply after money.
2. Used to be disgusted, now thinks there's a real element of skill in boxing. It's exciting.
3. Disgusting, brutal and sickening.

Task b

1. Parachuting.
2. A pub.
3. He's over 18.
4. Tense, because Steve and his father are arguing.
5. Steve: Approves of it; not too dangerous

   his father: Disapproves of it; extremely dangerous, a skill, expensive

   his mother: Approves of it; an excellent idea

   his sister Laura: Approves of it; exciting, fascinating

   his uncle John: Disapproves of it; terribly dangerous

Reference Key to Listening Tasks

Task c

Notes About the Talk:
The passage is about people called: sensation seekers
These people like: — strong emotions
— hard rock music
— extreme sports
— frightening horror movies
— danger
— risk
— excitement

Unit 18 Going on Holiday

Listening One

Task b

visiting my cousins	S	California	S
visiting friends	J	New York	J
camping	S	Washington	J
visiting museums	J	Boston	J
sailing	S	Great Lakes	J
going to rock concerts	J	New Orleans	S
surfing	S	Disneyworld	S
windsurfing	S	Youth Hostel	J
eating hamburgers	J		
eating hot dogs	J		
visiting the Empire State Building	J		

Task c

Weekend Special

Fare: $349

Leaves Detroit on Friday, Feb. 7 at 10:15 a.m.

Arrives in Miami at 1:00 p.m.

Leaves Miami on Sunday, Feb. 9 at /

Arrives in Detroit at /

7-Day Excursion

Fare: $324

Leaves Detroit on Mon.— Thur. at noon

Arrives in Miami at 3:45 p.m.

Leaves Miami on Mon. — Thur. at 3:00 p.m.

Arrives in Detroit at 6:45 p.m.

Night Flight

Fare: $299

Leaves Detroit on/at 11:00 p.m.

Arrives in Miami at 2:45 a.m.

Leaves Miami on/at/

Arrives in Detroit at/

Listening Two

Task a

Day one

Conditions: very cold, blocks of ice floating in river

Day two

Conditions: narrow part of the river, water moves fast, cold

Day three

What happened: One canoeist fell out of his canoe, managed to swim to shore. One walker fell over and broke his leg. He was taken to hospital by plane.

Conditions: little waterfall, a small lake

Reference Key to Listening Tasks

Days four and five

Conditions: wider and slower, scenery beautiful

Task b

a. 2)   b. 5)   c. 3)   d. 6)   e. 4)   f. 7)   g. 2)   h. 1)   i. 1)

Task d

1. Have at least 4 people in your party; Don't go hiking alone.
2. Expect the weather to get worse; Don't rely completely on weather forecasts.
3. Allow yourself plenty of time; Don't let darkness catch up with you.
4. Walk at the pace of the slowest member of your group; Don't leave anyone behind.
5. Before you start, tell people where you're going; Don't forget to tell them when you get back.
6. Plan your route before you set off; Take a map and a compass.
7. In your backpack carry some warm, water-proof clothing, and a first-aid kit.
8. Wear proper hiking boots—not sneakers ... or ... sandals.
9. Put emergency rations in your backpack.
10. Pack a flashlight in case you get caught in the dark.

Listening Test 1

Section One

1. Final discussion of urban pollution will move to Room 201.
2. Domestic shelter session will move to Room 304.
3. Return keys to the Porter's Lodge.
4. Return discussion records to the session chairpeople by five o'clock (5:00).
5. First coach for airport outside Kennedy Building at 15:30 (or 3:30).
6. Second coach at 17:15 (or 5:15). Delegates to arrive at least five (5) minutes before departure.
7. Dr. Schapsinger, Garbeldi and Surinander: collect reprints from the conference desk.
8. Dr. Goldman (Chicago Institute) 6th Annual Convention of P.E.S., in Hawaii, in October 1986. Interested parties leave your names at conference desk.

255

Section Two

Mr. Gibbon's Hobby: Stamp Collection

1. Age when he started collecting: <u>12</u>
2. Number of years collecting: <u>28</u>
3. First stamps: <u>British one, father gave him</u>
4. Size of stamp collection: <u>10,000</u>
5. Value of stamps: <u>15,000 pounds</u>
6. Oldest stamp: <u>Penny Black, British, 1840</u>
7. Countries collected: <u>GB, China, Finland</u>
8. Themes/subjects collected: <u>birds, animals, flowers, space travel</u>

Section Three

Call about aptment in Gazette

1. No. of bedrooms: <u>2</u>
2. Rent: <u>$425 a month</u>
3. Includes heat and electricity? <u>No</u>.
4. Average cost of utilities: <u>$35-$40 a month</u>
5. Washers/dryers in building? Yes.
6. Quiet building? <u>Yes</u>.
7. What floor? <u>2</u>nd.
8. Elevator? <u>No</u>.
9. Address: <u>44</u> Turner Drive
10. Near shopping? <u>Yes; 10 minutes walk away, or a couple of minutes by car</u>.
11. Who to see: <u>Marry Benevento, #31</u>
12. Time: <u>5:30</u>
13. Other information: <u>kitchen; living room; wall-to-wall carpeting; balcony; $50 deposit</u>

Listening Test 2

Section One

1. White Ghost.
2. Anyone. Better to be big multinational corporation.
3. Look around, upload or download some stuff.

4. It's fun./For fun.
5. Feel like I'm doing a public service.
6. Depends, all day or all night.
7. Alone.
8. Doesn't sell it.
9. It's top secret.

Section Two

1. year/spring
2. research
3. 250,000 pounds/a quarter of a million pounds
4. research award
5. proud
6. abnormal sleeping/nocturnal asthma
7. hay fever, the countryside

Section Three

1. People's memory and how far they could travel.
2. People listen to recorded music.
3. People become passive listeners of music./fewer and fewer people play musical instruments for fun.
4. Enriching the variety of music we hear,/people can hear music from different cultures.
5. An international style of music that combines different music types from all over the world.
6. *Graceland/Rhythm of the Saints/A World Out of Time*
7. It will weaken the traditional music of each country
8. Recording makes it possible for musicians to create new types of music and for us to have a wide variety of musical experiences.